AF553935

TEENAGER GIRLS AND THEIR PARENTS

TEENAGER GIRLS AND THEIR PARENTS

By

Dr. Neelma Kunwar
Deptt. of Extension Communication Management
Faculty of Home Science
C.S. Azad University of Agriculture & Technology
Kanpur (U.P.)

&

Dr. Swati Jain
B.A., M.A.
Deptt. of Home Science
NAKP Degree College
Chandausi

DISCOVERY PUBLISHING HOUSE PVT. LTD.
NEW DELHI-110 002

Published by:
Tilak Wasan
DISCOVERY PUBLISHING HOUSE PVT. LTD.
4831/24, Ansari Road, Prahlad Street
Darya Ganj, New Delhi-110002 (India)
Phone: +91-11-23279245, 43764432
Fax: +91-11-23253475
E-mail: parul.wasan@gmail.com
info@discoverypublishinggroup.com
web: www.discoverypublishinggroup.com

First Edition: **2011**
ISBN: 978-81-8356-728-2

Printed at:
Shree Balaji Art Press
Delhi

DEDICATED
to my Grand Parent and Parent

PREFACE

Much has been talked about a mothers closers for their serve while the daughter remains daddy's princess but the connection formed between a mother and her daughter is beyond any comparison. This book focuses on the sensitive relationship of the mother and daughter.

During adolescence parents and their sons and daughters must learn to establish new kinds of relationships with each other. Parents must be able to recognize and encourage the adolescents needs for increased, age-appropriate independence. Young people sequence sufficient from parental control to express themselves as individuals with needs and feelings of their own, to make decisions about their own lives and to take responsibility for the consequence of those decisions.

Most parents child interactions have later implications because the family is the setting in which each of us learns how to deal with other people. We come into the world ready to interact with other human beings. During the first year of life, when the range of possible behaviours is obviously limited, human infants are extremely sensitive to certain sounds facial expression and bodily movements. Human infants, are extremely sensitive to the specific sounds, facial expressions, and bodily movements of their care givers. And their care givers are equally sensitive to the infants sounds, expressions and movements. The result is interactive communication between mothers and infants.

Probably the best and most valued mother daughter relationship is the friendship kind. Such friendship based interactions between a mother and her daughter is less susceptible to tension and misunderstanding and there will be a lot of room for dialog rather than that of rushing to enforce authority. Both parties share their secrets freely between themselves and girls raised with such an interaction with their mothers tend to grow up to be confident and strong willed.

This book will help in understanding and building a better relationship between mother and her daughter, any constructive suggestion for improvement of the book will be gratefully received. The author expresses her indebtedness to the these Discovery Publishing House Pvt. Ltd., New Delhi for their painstaking efforts.

Authors

ACKNOWLEDGEMENTS

In this perishable world, there are still few things, which are imperishable. One of them is knowledge, not easy till one gets a mentor.

It is my proud privilege and great opportunity to work under such inspiring guidance and constructive criticism of Dr. Meenakshi Singh, Head (HDFS), Faculty of Home Science, Bundelkhand University, Jhansi. Her untiring supervision, persistent encouragement, unending zeal and conspicuous ability has always been a constant source of my achievement. I am extremely indebted to her for being meticulous throughout our investigation and preparation of this manuscript.

From the inner core of my heart, uncountable words of cordial veneration and gratitude are dedicated to the pious feet of my father Sri Anil Kumar Jain, my mother Smt. Suman Lata Jain for their love, affection, good wishes, blessings, constant encouragement and inspiration showed by them for the achievement of my present educational assets. I also express my warm appreciation to my brother Nikhil Kumar Jain, who extended moral support, timely help and constant inspiration to me during the entire period of my study.

It was difficult task for me to find appropriate words and express my sincere appreciation to my friends Ruchi, Surbhi & Anjali who helped me a lot during my research work.

Many more people who helped me directly or indirectly during course of studies, if I don't list them all, its not for lack of gratitude, it is lack of space. To them all, I convey my best compliments and lot of thanks.

With the blessing of almighty 'God', I am presenting this research work.

SWATI JAIN

CONTENTS

INTRODUCTION

Adolescence is an important stage in a child's development. Neither completely dependent nor wholly independent, adolescents occupy a middle ground in modern societies. It is during these years that individuals make significant investments in education, begin to shoulder responsibilities in the world of work, and are granted greater autonomy – behaviours that will have substantial long run consequences. Not surprisingly, research on adolescents has historically concentrated on academic achievement and transitions into adult roles. Of particular concern is how disadvantage, as measured by family structure, work environment, and parental education, impact such outcomes.

Most studies of youths' schooling have focused on outcomes such as test scores or highest grade completed. There has been much less research on the daily processes that give rise to these outcomes. However, given the availability of time–diary data, researchers have begun to examine the day-to-day activities of teenagers in more detail.

Empirical studies of teens' (and others') time use have been hampered by several significant limitations. First, many of the analyses have used aggregate measures of time use, such as daily minutes spent in a particular activity. Use of such aggregate measures, however, fails to utilize the detail available in time-diary data, which provide information on what activities are being performed and with whom every minute of the day. In contrast to this activities are being performed and with whom every minute of the day. In contrast to this approach, we examine the activities as spells and estimate competing risk hazard models of teenagers' continuation in and transitions out of these activities. A hazard approach is consistent with the way that the data are reported. The methodology also allows us to account for time-of 2-day effects, heaped reporting times, and other features of the data that aggregate studies necessarily overlook.

Second, a central research question regarding time use is how time devoted to one activity might crowd out time devoted to other activities. Thus, if disadvantaged teens are spending less time in schooling, research should address what they are doing instead. One possibility is that disadvantaged teens are devoting more time to housework or market labour. Another is that these teens take advantage of less supervision and pursue less structured schedules. Previous research has considered competing activities only in a limited way. Our methodology enforces an overall time constraint that allows us to see the trade-offs teenagers make.

ROLE OF MOTHER WITH RELATION TO TEENAGER GIRLS

Women have always worked to produce goods and services for themselves and their families. Every known economic system has been utilizing and presumably requiring work of women, they have been working in practically in every such system both for their maintenance and satisfaction as human beings and as members of society. Work done by women has included the processing and preparation of food and clothing, household care repair and similar household tasks.

For a child, a mother's role is very clearly defined. She is a care taker, a friend, a mentor, a chef, a chauffer, a doctor, a disciplinarian, a detective etc. A child's life is dictated by his mother's words and actions. She is a comfort giver and a primary source of identification for all children.

Much has been talked about a mother's closeness for their sons while the daughters remains daddy's princess but the connection formed between a mother and her daughter is beyond any comparison. She smears her lipstick, wears her high heels and tries to imitate her in every possible way. She's someone, the daughter aspires to become.

India is primarily an agricultural country and women working outside their homes are not a new phenomenon as they have been working in fields by the side of their men from time immemorial. The women from the economically least privileged strata of society have also been working since long for wages in factories as menial servants and as unskilled labourers.

The urban women of middle and upper classes especially the married women of these classes, whose taking up out of home gainful employment in comparatively a recent phenomenon.

Historically care of home and children has been allocated to the mother. The employment of the mother away from have and for any considerable time was believed to be incompatible with good care of home and children. Therefore, it was believed wrong for mothers to be employed outside of the home. The assumed neglect of home and children was not the only basis for objecting to employment of mothers. Many scholars earlier believed that the behaviour required in market place - aggressiveness, nationality, competitiveness were incompatible with rule requirements of mothers to be accepting nurturing and accommodating.

Today, there is a welcoming change from this attitude due to the rise in prices, education and standards of living. Women are joining work in large numbers. Most of the mothers are opting for work outside the home because of increase in literacy and importance of education. Most mothers want their children to have best in order to provide best to their children. Mothers are joining labour force. Alone all today the woman wants to stand on her own feet, she doesn't want to be dependent on anyone's shoulders.

PARENTAL RELATIONS AND THE DEVELOPMENT OF AUTONOMY

During adolescence parents and their sons and daughters must learn to establish new kinds of relationships with each other. Parents must be able to recognize and encourage – the adolescents' needs for increased, age-appropriate independence. Young people require sufficient freedom from parental control to express themselves as individuals with needs and feelings of their own, to make decisions about their own lives, and to take responsibility for the consequences of those decisions.

When parents continue to think of an adolescent as 'our darling baby' or 'our little boy' and treat him or her accordingly, they create a prescription for later problems in the form of explosive rebellion or inappropriate dependence. However, adolescents also need their parents' guidance and support, especially in early adolescence. The need for dependence continues to exist, often in an uneasy and fragile alliance with the need for greater independence. Partly because so many things are changing in the adolescent's world, the young person urgently needs a base of security and stability – something to take for granted while other, more immediate concerns are worked out.

Contrary to the arguments of some theorists, the development of age appropriate autonomy does not require that the adolescent abandon family ties. Indeed, under favourable circumstances the development of age appropriate autonomy is a dual process, providing both for separateness, individuality and self-exploration and for continuing family connectedness, encouragement.

As adolescence proceeds, there is a gradual shift away from unilateral parental authority toward more cooperative interactions. Although parents can – and do – continue to assert unilateral authority at times, particularly with respect to basic social obligations like schoolwork, in other matters (e.g. personal problems or concerns) they act as advisors who are willing to listen and seek to understand. In addition, adolescents spend much of their social and personal life outside the family circle, particularly with peers. Consequently, they are able to gain independence from parental authority in many more areas of their lives than is true for younger children.

FAMILY THE FIRST RELATIONSHIP WITH TEENAGERS

Most parent-child interactions have later implications because the family is the setting in which each of us learns how to deal with other people. We come into the world ready to interact with other human beings. During the first year of life, when the range of possible behaviours is obviously limited, human infants are extremely sensitive to certain sounds, facial expressions, and bodily movements. And most caregivers beginning early in their first year of life, human infants, are extremely sensitive to the specific sounds, facial expressions, and bodily movements of their caregivers (typically their mothers). And their caregivers are equally sensitive to the infant's sounds, expressions, and movements. The result is interactive communication between mother and infant.

ROLE OF MOTHER EMPLOYMENT WITH RELATIONSHIP

There are hundreds of studies comparing the children of working and non-working mothers. The cumulative findings are now fairly clear; for children past infancy, maternal employment has a generally positive effect for girls but sometimes is associated with negative effects for boys. Girls whose mothers work are more independent, have more positive views of the female role, and admire their mothers more than do girls whose mothers do not work. Boys whose mothers work also have more positive views of the female role, but in contrast to the findings for girls, boys whose mothers work are sometimes found to have lower academic achievement than do boys whose mothers stay home.

Most researchers in this area assume, as author does, that it is not employment *per se* that produces these effects, but rather that the mother's work creates changes both in the mother herself (her self-esteem or her morale, for example) and in the family's interaction patterns. But just what the specific links may be is still a matter of considerable debate. We do know that the mother's attitude toward her work or non work makes a difference. The most negative outcomes for children are typically found for two subgroups; mothers who would prefer to work but are staying at home and mothers who dislike their jobs or are unwilling workers. We also know that women who work have more decision making power within the family and they may also have higher self-esteem particularly if they are satisfied with their work. Such power of self-esteem may spill over particularly into the woman's interaction with her children, perhaps especially with a daughter. Bronfenbrenner finds, for example that working mothers give more positive descriptions of their young daughters than do non-working mothers, which may help to account for the more positive outcomes for girls whose mothers are employed. But these connections are still tentative.

Father's Employment

Older research on the impact of father's work on family life focused on unemployment. It is only very recently that psychologists have begun to look for more subtle kinds of connections between family interactions and the father's work satisfaction, his particular job demands, or work values. So I can only give you fragments.

In families in which the mother is employed full-time, the father is usually more involved in housework and child rearing than fathers in more traditional families, although domestic responsibilities are seldom divided equally. Nevertheless, children who live in a home where both parents are employed experience a more egalitarian relationship between the parents, more care by people outside the family, and more responsibility for household chores than children in other types of family.

WORKING MOTHER'S RELATIONSHIP

Because household operations have become more efficient and family size has decreased in India, it is not certain that children with mothers working outside the home actually receive less attention than children in the past whose mothers were not employed outside the home. Outside employment – at least for mothers with school – aged children – may simply be filling time previously taken up by added household burdens and more children. It also cannot be assumed that, if the mother did not go to work, the child would benefit from the time freed by streamlined household operations and smaller families.

Mothering does not always have a positive effect on the child. The educated, non-working mother may over invest her energies in her children, fostering an excess of worry and discouraging the child's independence. In such situations, the mother may inject more parenting than the child can profitably handle. While a mother's employment is not associated with negative child outcomes, a certain set of children from working mother families bear further scrutiny – those called latchkey children. They typically do not see their parents from the time they leave for school in the morning until about 6.00 or 7.00 p.m. They are called latchkey children because they are given the key to their home, they take the key to school, and then they use it to let themselves into the home while their parents are still at work. Latchkey children are largely unsupervised for two to four hours a day during each school week. During the summer months, they may be unsupervised for entire days, five days a week.

MATERNAL EMPLOYMENT AND CHILD DEVELOPMENT

Children of mothers who enjoy their work and remain committed to parenting show very favourable adjustment – a higher sense of self-esteem, more positive family and peer relations, less gender stereotyped beliefs, and better grades in school. Girls, especially, profit from the image of female competence. African - American adolescent girls whose mothers worked during the daughter's early years are more likely to stay in school. And overall, daughters of employed mothers perceive the woman's role as involving more freedom of choice and satisfaction and are more achievement and career oriented.

These benefits undoubtedly result from parenting practices. Employed mothers who value their parenting role are more likely to use authoritative child rearing and co-regulation – granting their child independence with oversight. Also, children in dual-earner households devote more daily hours to doing housework under parental guidance and participate more in household chores. And maternal employment results in more time with fathers, who take on greater child care responsibility. More paternal contact is related to higher intelligence and achievement, mature social behaviour and gender-stereotype flexibility.

However, when employment places heavy demands on the mother's schedule, children are at risk for ineffective parenting. Working long hours and spending little time with children are associated with less favourable adjustment. In contrast, part time employment seems to have benefits for children of all ages, probably because it prevents work overload, thereby helping mothers meet children's needs.

INTERDEPENDENT RELATIONSHIPS WITH FAMILY AND FRIENDS VERSUS LONELINESS

The common element of all close relationships is interdependence, an interpersonal association in which two people consistently influence each other's lives, focus their thoughts and emotions on one another, and regularly engage in joint activities whenever possible. Close relationships with friends, family members, and one's spouse also include an element of commitment. Interdependence occurs across age groups and across quite different kinds of interactions.

The affection of mothers for their offspring appears to be based, at least in part, on hormones. Do other interpersonal bonds also rest on biological factors? There is good reason to believe that our need for companionship has evolutionary roots. DNA evidence indicates that, among other species, chimpanzees and bonobos are our closest evolutionary relatives, and they are more closely related to us than to gorillas or orangutans.

Keeping in view the above facts, the present study has, therefore, been designed to investigate the "Teenager's girls and their interpersonal relationship with their working and non-working mothers" with the following specific objectives:

OBJECTIVES

1. To study the socio-demographic people of teenager's girls.
2. To knowledge the nature, attitude and relationship of teenager's with her working and non-working mothers.
3. To identify the responsibility and role of teenager's in household activities with selected mothers.
4. To understand interpersonal relationship between mothers and girls. Patterns of interaction between mothers and girls.
   (a) Sharing of experiences and activities
   (b) Knowledge of friends
   (c) Discipline maintained of different level with mothers.
   (d) Personal problems.

LIMITATIONS OF THE STUDY

In most of the researches examined the emphasis was centered on infants, preschoolers, children at grade school levels. Issues concerning the impact on children in middle childhood and adolescent are generally neglected and were not considered a crucial area of research. We argue, however that children in late middle childhood and early adolescence are likely to face significant challenges with regard to their relationship with their mothers. Our study is based on teenager girls because teenager's is a developmental epoch characterized by rapid physical, intellectual, socio-emotional growth and change, which is frequently accompanied by turbulence, perplexity and confusion.

Hence, this study is undertaken specifically to examine the relationship of teenage girls with their working and non-working mothers. Today, mothers are also stepping out of their homes and are earning a living for themselves and their families. They are becoming independent. Now working has become a social need and is contributing towards upliftment of women.

REVIEW OF LITERATURE

Review of literature is very important for any type of research work. A brief review of available literature is presented in the chapter, which provides a basis for the theoretical framework and interpretation of findings.

Fisher and Tronto (1990), the effects of scheduling on mothers. All of these mothers were asked they were satisfied with the way their lives were going.

Steinberg (1990) changes in family relationships during the adolescent years are often thought to be characterized by increases in both conflict and emotional characterized by increases in both conflict and emotional distance between parents and their adolescent children.

Ilyas (1990) found that virginity and good upbringing of the daughters is the most important concern for the working mothers and consequently they experience anxiety and role conflict.

Crouter *et al.* (1990) parents who did not closely monitor their activities earned poorer grades than more closely monitored children.

Rower (1991) no significant differences were found between adolescents self esteem scores of adolescent daughters of both working and non-working mothers.

Starrels (1992) found that adolescent females of mothers employed full time expressed significantly greater approval of maternal employment than did those whose mothers were not employed.

Mates and Allison (1992) when children enter this age group, they may suddenly find the world unfolding for them, which can be a decidedly mixed blessing because of the many opportunities they have to engage in risky behaviour such as neglecting school or becoming sexually active or involved with drugs, gangs and violence.

Hoffman (1993) the new study also finds that sons as well as daughters of working mothers had higher scores on standardized achievement teats in reading, match and science.

Richardson (1993) teenagers may like being frees to direct their own activities when their mothers are out of the house. However, with less supervision adolescents are more susceptible to peer pressure. Children who are unsupervised after school tend to smoke, drink use marijuana or engage in other risky behaviour, to be depressed and to have low grades.

Brown (1993) the extent to which parents monitored adolescent's behaviour and school work, encouraged achievement, and allowed joint decision-making were related to academic achievement, self reliance. These behaviours in turn, were linked with membership in peer groups.

Christopher *et al.* (1993) examined children who have more household responsibilities may actually have less parental monitoring. That is their parents may be home less often and thus the children take on more adult roles. The parents especially mothers who spend more time supervising their children have children who engage in fewer risky behaviour.

Lloyd (1994) studied the unemployed mothers especially those without outside help and support tend to become depressed and depressed mothers tended to be negative in their perception of maternal role and punitive with their children. Young people who saw their relationships with their mothers deteriorate tended to be depressed themselves and to have trouble in school.

Nock and Kingston (1995) states that most employed parents work longer hours than parent did 20 years ago. As a result they have little time to spend with their children. To make matters worst, if there are two working parents in one household, that family may receive no institutional support. According to the Family and Medical Leave Act, legislative support for working parents is limited to maternity leaves or leaves for family illness. The school system offers programmes for preschoolers and after-school activities for elementary school children. Once children reach middle school, parents find few after-school programmes geared to their needs.

Ruddick (1995) says care as "labour and relationship", she has in mind the mundane work feeding, cleaning, and transporting children. We argue that counseling and training of adolescents is also a form of caring labour. If Ruddick's analysis is applied to the care work of parents with teenagers, we can explain some seeming contradictions in the relationships between parents and young teenagers in our study. Ruddick's thesis suggest that parents' efforts to train and counsel their teenage children take place within the historical and emotional context of the relationship, a context that colours and shapes the perceptions they and their children have about the children's needs.

Paulson *et al*. (1990) have studied parenting strategies. Becker and Moen's (1999) study does not focus specifically on parents of adolescents, but their review of the recent literature on parenting strategies is important for this study because it emphasizes the ways in which family members actively construct and modify their roles, resources and relationships by constructing various adaptive strategies (see also Goode 1960; Moen and Wethington 1992). Becker and Moen cite studies that have identified a broad range of coping strategies and repertories, including gender and life-stage differences in individual coping styles (for example, see, Skinner and McCubbin 1991; Schnittger and Bird 1990; Gilbert 1988), Becker and Moen's (1999) own research on 117 parents in dual earner households found that the great majority were engaging in "scaling back" strategies that helped the couples reduce and restructure their commitment to paid work, thereby buffering them from work encroachment. The authors' findings suggest that gender and life-course factors shape work family strategies – wives disproportionately scaled back; some husbands and wives trade off family and career responsibilities at different life stages. Those in the early childbearing phase were more apt to scale back than parents with older children. Becker and Moen's study raises important questions about the strategic choices of some dual earner couples and moves us beyond the focus on maternal employment and its consequences for adolescent development.

Dornbusch (1995) says that children who had authoritative parents are lese likely to misbehave in school and less susceptible to antisocial peer pressure, girls are more self reliant and work oriented, had higher self-esteem and are less likely to be anxious or depressed.

Tarlow (1996) says the essence of care is an emotional bond, but point out that neither the feelings of love and concern alone nor the mere physical work of reproducing and maintaining life are enough in and of themselves to constitute care. Rather, both the physical and the emotional must coexist. Tarlow also suggests, even when they were "exhausted and just wiped out with swollen feet", as Eleanor says when describing how she felt at the end of day just before she began tackling her daughter's homework assignments.

Gavin (1996) examined factors associated with harmony in adolescent girls' relationships with their mothers and their best friends. A framework was proposed in which relationship harmony was expected to be related to individual characteristics of each partner and the match between the individual characteristics of each partner. Sixty adolescent girls, their mothers and their best friends participated in self-report and observational tasks. Harmonious mother-daughter partners (vs. disharmonious ones) had more similar needs, felt their needs were better met, perceived their partners as more socially skilled and had more similar interests. Harmonious friends (vs. disharmonious ones) had more similar needs, and target adolescents perceived partners to be more socially skilled and better at meeting their needs. Observational ratings of attunement, positive affect, and power negotiation were greater in harmonious relationships with both mothers and friends. Discussion focuses on the value of a common framework for studying different relationships.

Arnedell (1997) recognized that, in general, there is a crisis of care for middle schoolers who do not have any adult care, and the evidence is clear that some teenagers suffer from a care shortage; it is not clear, however, how working parents perceive and resolve the challenging tasks of caring for their young teenagers.

Kiuchi (1997) observed that the students were influenced by "past school life" in contrast with their mothers who were influenced by "family". On conflicts over the demand from a situation, both the students and mothers who gave priority to interdependent construal of the self tended to feel conflicts when the situation demanded them to act independently. On the other hand, SS who gave priority to independent construal of the self tended to feel conflicts when the situation demanded them to act interdependently.

Miller *et al.* (1997) examined the transmission of parental bonding style from 60 mothers and 69 daughters. Result showed that a series of logistic regressions were run to predict daughter report of maternal affectionless control, taking into account maternal and daughter depression status, temperament and socio-economic status. Results show that the intergenerational transmission of parental bonding among SS was shown to be independent of maternal depression, daughter depression, maternal temperament, daughter temperament and socio-economic status. However, results suggest that a daughter's temperament may be a risk factor for parental affectionless control.

Hochschild (1997) suggest, provides us with a model to focus on the everyday strategies required to perform care while preserving intimacy. We argue that parents face a set of particular problems in caring for teenagers' ages 12 to 14 years-old. Principal among these is the contested nature of their need for care. The workplace continues to demand a total commitment and to force people who are immersed in their careers to place their parenting second. In its demands, as this study suggests, the work world is dependent on a dominant perception of adolescents as self-sufficient young adults and not adolescents who still need a log of parental love and support. If, therefore, we want our young teenagers to get the care they need and deserve, the battles must be fought to the workplace to allow even successful career workers limit their time at work. As it stands now, and as the parents in this study suggest, there is an unequal division of physical and emotional care, and that inequality has implications for the emotional life of many families. Also states that emotion work involves the following behaviour; attending carefully to how a setting affects others in it – through taking the role of the other and feeling some of the same feelings; focusing attention through ruminating about the past and planning for the future; assessing the reasonableness of preliminary judgments by checking over the behaviour by checking over the behaviour of all respondents in an interaction – just as good hostesses do when they look for signs of how well people are enjoying a party, whether or not anyone appears ill at ease or left out; creating a comfortable ambience through expressions of gaiety, warmth, sympathy, and cheerful, affectionate concern for or interest in another. Emotion work is an example of how gender expectations and the privacy sphere are interconnected in a job description, for it is women's job in our society to manage these tasks in the family.

Hochschild (1998) says care as labour intensive emotional bond work that requires physical as well as emotional labour, at least on the part of the caregiver, in which the care giver feels responsible for others' well-being and does mental, emotional, and physical work in the course of fulfilling that responsibility in the context of intimacy. For example, in this study, it would be that one parent has to tolerate the non-supportive attitude of the other parent just before driving a "grouchy" eighth grader to school or the parent may have to contend with the mood swings of a 12-year old while packing her or his lunch. Our second objective is to focus on the everyday strategies required to perform care while preserving intimacy.

Dekovic *et al*. (1998) found teens of mothers who moved from non-employment to employment saw anxiety and teens of mothers who went from employment to non-employment saw increased behaviour problems.

Hoffman (1998) in contrast with full time homemakers, employed mothers differentiate less between sons and daughters in their discipline style and in their goals for their children. Hoffman also say twenty years ago, it would have seemed strange to give a talk on maternal employment and not focus on it as a social problem, but there is little in these data to suggest it is. The mother's employment status does have effects on families and children, but few of these effects are negative one's. Indeed, most seem positive – the higher academic outcomes for children, benefits in their behavioural conduct and social adjustment, and the higher sense of competence and effectiveness in daughters. On the whole, these research results suggest that most families accommodate to the mother's employment and in doing so provide a family environment that works well.

Gottfried (1999) show that positive effects of maternal employment are multiplied when fathers contribute to childcare and household responsibilities.

Bluestone and Monda (1999) mothers of adolescent cut back on their social, educational and other uses of time away from their teenagers to make up for the loss of time spent away because of work.

Grader and Brooks (1999) studied conflict and closeness in mother – daughter relationships and the ways in which these 2 relational dimensions are associated with girls development, as a function of pubertal status and onset of sexuality. Results showed that some conflict is not only normative, but may be growth enhancing conflict and disagreements may be the context in which girls learn negotiation or bargaining.

Mills (1999) examined the mother's beliefs about the balance of power in the parent child relationship and the influence these beliefs may have on their management of parent-child conflict and their children's socio-emotional adjustment. Findings suggest that maternal percentins of low power in the context of a power advantage may predict subsequent maternal over control but not internatizing symptoms.

Camacho and Wanda (1999) examined the impact of a graduate level of education on the relationship between Puerto Rican mothers and daughters. Result showed that the daughter's degree of education would have an impact on her personal development, integration into the dominant culture and social status. Predictably, the interconnection between mothers and daughters from disparate educational background would be influenced by these areas of adjustment.

Powers and Welsh (1999) considered that the mother daughter interactions and adolescent girls symptoms of depression, specifically, the proposition that adolescent depression is associated with difficulties in interpersonal behaviours that facilitate individuation. They suggest that conflict may be necessary occurrence your optimal out comes during specific developmental phases of transitions.

Becker and Moen (1999) and Hochschild (1997) have contributed to the research on parents' adaptative methods, but this study finds that often there is a conflict between what parents want to do as parents and what they need to do as career-minded professionals. Most parents admitted to experiencing a great deal of conflict over caring for a teenager, satisfying their obligations to the other parent, and, at the same time pursuing their own careers.

Enberg (1999), putting family first in an ambitious, career-minded society can be a very difficult, an even passed, decision. Young women contemplating marriage, motherhood and work need a helpful guide to understanding and meeting the challenges of work and family. Those who have sacrificed career dreams in the face of motherhood are especially in need of reassurance. This is the author's urgent call for women to negotiate equality in the home and for men to understand that motherhood and "housework" are just as important as breadwinning. In pithy and hard-hitting chapters, using hilarious and hair-raising personal experiences, she challenges the studies and assertions of "experts" who fail to address family issues in realistic, or realizable, terms. She offers fresh points of view and advice for women on youthful decision making, parenting, handling teenagers, finance and much more. Emphasizing a feminine individualism and forecasting the highs and lows of family work life.

Garey (1999) says that several women, like Eleanar and Jeannie, the scheduler for example agreed with that assumption. Eleanar see the issue of daughter care as one primarily affecting women – I have a (women) friend with three kids, and we give each other little bullet support because we are both so stressed out.

Kaplan (2000) on teenage boys suggest that adolescents still have much of the emotional vulnerability of children, and, like children, they suffer in the absence of parental love and supervision. This is true despite their larger size, their greater autonomy in moving around, and their increasing powers of abstract thinking. Consequently, parents develop different kinds of care strategies to supervise and guide children during the "beautiful but dangerous" stage of their lives. As their offsprings grow, parents discover that their "cute" and dependent child has grown into a 12 or 13-year old with a point of view and with the capability to organize his or her own activities. Children continue to need care as they mature but in less tangible ways than when they were younger. Young teenagers demand to be understood, paid attention to, and sympathized with, even though they can usually fix their own meals, the caregiver is a rational actor, her goal is to get an accurate sense of the needs of the person she is looking after and to muster all the resources at her disposal in order to meet those needs. From this perspective, a mother continues to care for her child after she or he becomes a teenager, but transforms the kind of caring work.

Weiss (2000) say children get older and become teenagers the intensive physical work of caring tends to diminish, and parents expend more of their efforts on caring-as-relationship. And because social scientists tend to be skittish about studying emotions, scholars of care have largely ignored the caring relationships between parents and young teenagers. Most studies on dual-earner parents of adolescents examine the effect of the mothers' employment on adolescent development.

Furstenberg (2000) says additional research on the benefits and consequences of young employment, examined changes in adolescents' work and other activities over time. She found that recent cohorts of teens spend substantially less time in paid employment than teens in the 1970s. However, the time freed from working has not led to more time in school or other enriching activities. Instead, time spent in passive leisure activities has increased.

Bianchi (2000) says that maternal employment may also lead to a loss of social capital in neighbourhood, as parents are likely to get together and watch each others children.

Hoffman (2000) states that daughters of employed mothers perceive the women's role as involving more freedom of choice and satisfaction and more achievement and career oriented.

Lee (2000) examined the mother-daughter relationship, expected and acceptable achievement norms, the impact of a working mother, the mother as role model, daughters perceptions of themselves as functioning adolescents/adults, how mothers cope with conflict between ethnic values and perceived goals and their definitions of success. Findings concerning early recognition of talent, personality traits of mothers, influence of social support and stress, families, parenting and social mobility across generations are presented.

Pecchioni and Nussbaum (2000) examined the attitudes of older, independent mothers and their adult daughters and their communication behaviour during decision making regarding care giving preferences. Results show that older mothers held stronger beliefs in paternalism. Daughters beliefs did not change with their own age or that of their mothers. Both groups of Ss reported strong beliefs in shared autonomy. Daughter talked more, taking control of conversations from their mothers. Autonomy and paternalism scores were not predicted by the extent daughters spoke for their mother or appeared to be decision makers. Findings suggest that Ss attitudes toward paternalism influenced who controlled conversations regarding potential care giving.

Gross and Maccallum (2000) studied the mothers and adolescent daughters synchrony was achieved by using the mother daughter synchrony scale (MDSS) developed for this study. Synchrony is defined as the quality and quantity of communication, support and harmony between mother and daughter. Synchrony between mother and daughter, as perceived by the daughter, was significantly related to the daughter's self esteem and academic competence. Further more a hierarchical regression analysis showed that synchrony was a moderate predictor of grade point average after partialing out variance because of self-esteem.

Duncan (2001) states both parents including mothers employment may create stress in the family by reducing parents opportunities to spend time with their children and interfering with parents monitoring of their children's activities.

Morris and Ramanan (2001) states that during adolescent period, parents and teenagers report feeling less close to one another as they spend less time together.

Blum, R.W. (2002) says parents need to know their teens' friends and speak with their friends' parents. Most importantly, teens and especially younger teens, who feel close to their mothers, are less likely to start having sex. Findings from other Add Health research have also shown that teens whose parents value education are less likely to have sex.

Andrew (2002) studied the working mothers came to believe, that her increased work responsibilities left her less able to supervise her teen and contributed to her child's problem in school.

Washington, (2002) say teenagers are less likely to start having sex when their mothers are involved in their lives, have a close relationship with them, and stress and importance of education, according to new findings from the largest survey ever conducted with adolescents in the United States. The results were most consistent among younger teens in the eighth and ninth grades. But simply warning teenagers about the dangers of early sex or telling them that they shouldn't have sex does not stop them from becoming sexually active, the study researchers found. The latest results from the National Longitudinal Surveys on Adolescent Health (Add Health) draw from interviews with more than 3,000 pairs of mothers and their teens. The findings were reported today in a monograph by University of Minnesota researchers and in the Journal of Adolescent Health.

Kaplan (2002), Thirty working parents interviewed for the study offer three unique strategies for raising teenagers ages 12 to 14 years old by Kalpan (2002). This study draws on the literature on care and on parents' perception of their teenagers' needs, on their own abilities to perform the necessary caring tasks, and on their appraisals of their spouses' commitments to caring for their teenagers. Rather than produce strategies that are based on negotiations with family members, parents in this study tended to develop their own individual strategies when confronted with a set of problems in caring for young teenagers, principle among these is the contested nature of teenagers' need for care-contested by the educational institution, by employers, by spouses and teenagers themselves. We conclude by suggesting that these parents' strategies lead to unequal divisions of physical and emotional care that are shaped by gender, race and institutional intransigence.

Moffitt (2003) studied teenage children would benefit because mothers who worked and were off welfare would increase their income and would have more structured home life as well as be a better role model for their children.

Abraham and Villanueva (2005) examined the mother – daughter relationships and conflict specifically develops over a 3-year period. The sample included African American, European American and Latina girls and mothers. Results indicate American– African and Latina mothers reported significantly higher levels of disciplinary behaviours at both assessments, mothers and daughters from all ethnicities reported positive, nurturant relationship, neither pubertal status nor timing directly predicted conflict, but timing and conflict were moderated by ethnicity. Finally, conflict during late-childhood was associated with adolescent adjustment during early adolescence.

Bowles (2005) says greater household need in the form of a larger household or more young siblings may also increase the demands on teenagers' time. In their review of the consequences of welfare-to work programmes on adolescents' development.

Gennetian *et al.* (2002) found that adolescent children of welfare recipients who had younger siblings experienced larger negative effects on school performance, and were more likely to be suspended or expelled from and to drop out of school, than adolescent children of welfare recipients who were not subject to such policies.

Call *et al.* (1995) reported that household size was an important predictor of the time teenagers spent in housework and care activities.

Bronfenbrenner and Morris (2005) says that children of employed mothers tend to live in more structured homes with clear cut rules giving them more household responsibilities. They are encouraged to be more independent. Independence helps girls to become more competent, to achieve more in school and to have higher self-esteem than children of full time home makers.

Lewis Jane (2007) says two recent reports, from the ippr and UNICEF have provided disturbing evidence on the behaviour and well-being of young people in the UK. The ippr's Report suggests that a significant explanatory factor is a lack of time children spend with parents and other adults. But is mere 'presence' the key? The paper briefly reviews the possibilities parents in the UK have to spend time with their children by exploring how much and when they work in relation to parents in other European countries, and goes on to report on evidence from interviews with parents and children, which signal the importance of parenting style. I suggest that time with children is not unimportant, which has implications for Government's decision not to extend the right to request flexible working patterns to parents with older children, but that it is far from being the only factor at stake. The increasing difficulties parents face in negotiating the transition to independence with their teenage children indicate a need for parenting to be on the policy agenda.

Price *et al.* (2007) found that teenagers with a single parent go to bed later and are less likely to eat dinner with a parent. They also found that teens with more educated parents spend more time studying and less time watching TV, are more likely to eat dinner with a parent, and get less sleep. An increase in work among disadvantaged teens, which Price et al. also found, might increase their independence and disrupt parents' ability to supervise their teens. However, in a study limited to two-parent families.

Porterfield and Winkler (2007) found that teen time use differs relatively little across different types of families, they found that such time use does vary markedly by race, ethnicity, and parental education, which may also proxy for disadvantaged circumstances. For example, they found that parental education is positively associated with teenagers' homework time.

Marshall (2007) found that family environment is a strong predictor of time spent in homework by Canadian teens, with teens more likely to do homework and more of it if both parents had a university education, and if they lived in a two parent, intact family. She also found that teens with demanding paid jobs did significantly less homework than those who were not employed.

Kalenkoski and Pabilonia (2009) parents positively affects homework time, having a more-educated mother negatively affects screen time, and living with a single parent reduces homework time. While the above-mentioned time-diary studies have tried to determine how teenagers' daily activities are affected by family circumstances, these studies suffer from several limitations. First, they rely on analyses of total daily time spent in various activities but do not separately account for the incidence and duration of activities. Second, they do not account for the timing and interdependence of different activities. Third, they do not account for the daily time constraint that requires that additional time spent in one activity must reduce time spent in at least one other activity. Our event-history approach addresses all of these issues.

Crepinsek and Rurstein (2009) compared with children of non-working mothers, children of full-time working mothers have lower overall HEI (Healthy Eating Index) scores, lower intake of iron and fiber, and higher intake of soda and fried potatoes, even after taking into account differences in maternal and other family characteristics. Nutritional differences between children of part-time working mothers and children of non-working mothers were more sensitive to maternal and family characteristics, with no clear pattern of nutritional differences emerging. This study analyzed differences in nutrition outcomes among children whose mothers work full time, part time, and not at all, and the role USDA's Child and Adult Care Food Programme (CACFP) plays in meeting the nutrition needs of participating children, especially those whose mothers work.

PROFILE OF THE STUDY AREA

Prior to discuss the findings of the study, it is essential to sketch briefly the salient features of the study area. The following are the brief features of district Moradabad.

DISTRICT MORADABAD

The area covered by the present district Moradabad lay, in early times, is the northwestern part of what was known as the country of Panchala, which is said to have extended from the Himalayas in the north to the river Chambal in the south. Later, when Panchala was divided into two parts, this area was included in north Panchala which had its capital of Achichchatra (in the Bareilly district, a few kilometres from eastern border of the Moradabad district). On the west of the district, across the Ganga, lay the country of the Kurus, the close allies of the panchalas, with their capital at Hastinapur (in the Meerut district).

In the closing centuries of the first millennium of the Christian are the entire region including the Moradabad district (which lies west of Awadh between the Himalayas and the Ganga) came to be know as Katehr, a name replaced only towards the middle of the eighteenth century by the term of Rohilkhand, the district forming the west-central portion of the region so designated.

CLIMATE

Climate of the district is hot in summer season and much cold and dry in winter season because it lies in the *tarai* region of Himalayas.

AREA

Out of the total geographical area of 5,96,700 square metre, agriculture is being done on only 4,87,243 hectares. Normally, in 3,10,086 hectares area *Kharif*, in 3,97,070 hectares area *Rabi* and 25,441 hectares area *Zaid* crops are grown, purely irrigated area in the district is 3,92,000 hectares. Irrigation is done through canals, government and private tube wells. Paddy, *Jowar, bajra, mung, urd, arhar* in *Kharif* and wheat, barley, gram and pea is cropped in Rabi season in the district, sugarcane, potato and menthe is grown and sent to the market at Delhi.

POPULATION

Population of the district Moradabad is 14,15,424 males and 12,31,867 females as per the 2001 census and the selected tehsil Chandausi the total population is 2,34,084 in which there are 1,26,816 males and 1,07,298 are females.

SELECTION OF SCHOOLS AND COLLEGES

Hundred Ten teenager girls working mothers and 110 teenager's girls non-working mother were selected in different schools and colleges. Thus, total 220 respondents were selected in this study.

RESEARCH METHODOLOGY

This chapter deals with the research procedures applied in conducting the present study. For convenience, the research methodology has been discussed under the following three sub-heads:-

Locale of the study

(i) District under study

(ii) Selection of teenagers

(iii) Pre-testing of instrument

Variables and their operationalization

(i) Independent variables

(ii) Dependent variables

Data gathering procedure and statistical technique used

(i) Data collection

(ii) Period of investigation

(iii) Statistical techniques.

LOCALE OF THE STUDY

Uttar Pradesh was chosen as locale of the study. This was done with the intension that U.P. is a major State of the country and teenager girls have an important role to play in the development of the State as well as the country.

(i) District under study

District Moradabad was purposively selected for this study as the researcher hailed from this place. This helped the investigator to collect the necessary information accurately and timely. The researcher, being from the same place could easily have dialogues and discussions with both during pilot study and final data collection.

(ii) Selection of teenagers

From each selected sample, 110 teenager girls with working mothers and 110 teenager girls with non-working mothers. A total number of 220 teenagers with working and non-working mothers were selected for the study area.

(iii) Pre-testing of instruments

In accordance with the methodological procedures related with various variables to attain the specific objectives of the investigation, interview schedule was developed for the data collection. The schedule so developed was pre-tested on 220 teenager girls. On the basis of the responses obtained from the 220 teenager girls during pre-testing modification alterations, additions deletions were made so as to have a well constructed, functional, manageable and workable schedule and scientific tool

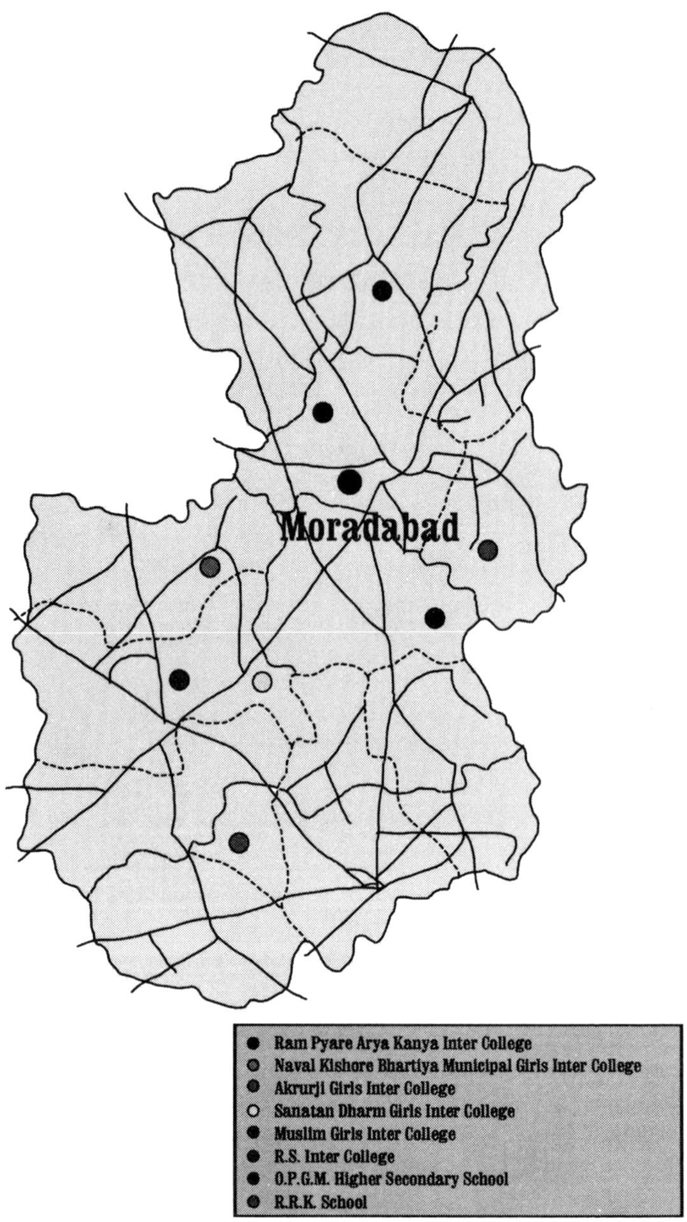

Fig. 4.1: Moradabad District

for data collection. With the help of duly pre-tested interview schedule, specific data were collected. The interview schedule was administered individually by the research and responses were obtained. Subsequently, the recorded responses were analysed statistically to draw meaningful inferences.

VARIABLES AND THEIR OPERATIONALIZATION

Socio-economic Features

It describes the position of an individual or a family occupied with reference to the prevailing average possessions and participation in the group activities of the community.

In view of this, the socio-economic features of the teenager girls in the present study was operationalized in term of independent variables like age, education, type of family, caste, occupation, economic status, etc. and dependent variables.

OPERATIONALIZATION OF THE VARIABLES

Independent variables

Age

Age is defined as the chronological age of respondents in form of number of completed years. It was measured as per scoring system followed in socio-economic status scale of Trivedi (1963) with certain modification.

Table 4.1: Age

Age-group (years)	Score assigned
13 - 14	1
15 - 16	2
17 - 18	3

Caste

Caste of the respondents in the study was measured on the basis of response of individual girls to which they belong, i.e.

in terms of upper caste, backward caste and schedule caste/ schedule tribe. The scores were assigned as in Table 4.2.

Table 4.2: Caste

Caste	Score assigned
Upper caste (General)	1
Other backward caste (OBC)	2
Schedule caste/Scheduled tribe (SC/ST)	3

Religion

The selected study area was having mostly Hindu religion and some are Muslim. The following table 4.3 shows scoring pattern was adopted.

Table 4.3: Religion

Category	Score assigned
Hindu	1
Muslim	2
Sikh	3
Christian	4

Family Structure

Family composition was scored on the basis of family type and family members (Table 4.4).

Table 4.4: Family Structure

(a) According of family type	Score assigned
Nuclear family	1
Joint family	2

(b) According to family members	Score assigned
2 to 4 members	1
5 to 7 members	2
8 and above members	3

Economic Status

The position of an individual or a family occupies to the prevailing average standards of cultural possession, effective income, material possession and participation in the group activity of the community.

Economic status of the respondents in this study were lower, middle and middle and high. The following scoring pattern was adopted (Table 4.5).

Table 4.5: Economic Status

Economic status	Score assigned
Lower	1
Middle	2
Higher	3

Income

The annual monetary income of the respondents were assessed and scores were assigned as shown a Table 4.6.

Table 4.6: Annual Income

Income of working mother	Score assigned
Up to Rs. 5,000	1
Rs. 5,000 to 10,000	2
Rs. 10,000 to 15,000	3
Rs. 15,000 and above	4

Dependent Variables

Attitude

Attitude is considered as an important component of human behaviour. Thus, for the purpose of study, it was conceptualized as teenager girls. Therefore, attitude was taken as an independent variable in the present study.

Knowledge

Knowledge for the purpose of the study referred to the amount of correct information possessed by respondents regarding various aspects of relation of teenager girls with mothers.

Awareness

Awareness is variously defined, in this study. It is a measure of target women who were aware about their health and nutrient intake. It comprises a human's perception and cognitive reaction to a condition or event. Awareness does not necessarily imply understanding. It is just an ability to be conscious of feel or perceive.

Peer

The peer group, like the family group, is a primary group with immediate, face to face, close association. As the child grows the norms of the peer group may largely determine what behaviour is accepted or rejected, approved or disapproved. The peer group provides a degree of emotional support for most children, they may get more understanding from the friends than even from the parents.

Disciplining

Discipline is often considered as essential for the growth and development of child. In the absence of discipline, the child's world remains too "unstructured" to permit adjustment. If there are no rules to the game of living, a child will not be able to learn to play it. It is a very important instrument in the process of socialization in which parents guide the child in the direction of what is socially acceptable in his/her culture.

Parent-Child Relationship

Parental attitudes towards the child affect his/her self-concept. Pattern of parental reward the punishment for child's behaviour is crucial in the development of child's self-concept. If parental discipline does not satisfy the needs of the developing child, child may develop negative personality characteristics. Parents may be detached, indifferent, neglecting rejecting, over protective and indulgent and possessive. Parents may be liberal, cooperative, accepting, sufficiently protective and controlling. Any combination of these characteristics is possible. Many psychologists observe that children with high self-esteem tend to have parents who are also high in self-esteem. Such parents show consistency in encouraging and supporting their children. Such parents are self-confident emotionally stable, self reliant, resilient, effective in their child rearing practices, and compatible with each other. Mothers of such children are more accepting and supportive, expressing their acceptance through everyday manifestations of concern and affection. These mothers also enforce established rules consistently, preferring rewards and non-coercive treatment in efforts to alter their children's behaviour.

Parenting Style

Parenting style is a constellation of attitude toward the child that are communicated to the child and create an emotional climate or context in which concrete parenting practices are expressed and in which adolescent development takes place. An example of such parenting style is authoritative parenting a constellation of emotional support or involvement, high standards or firm control and very low levels of psychological control. Many studies have indicated that authoritative parenting is most adapting for young adolescent's psychological adjustment. However, other studies showed that authoritative parenting is associated with lower levels of emotional autonomy in the adolescent.

Career Aspiration

Adolescence is a critical time for forming career aspiration. School performance which has psychological concomitants, is the key mechanism through which adolescent learn about their talent abilities and competencies which are an important part of developing career aspirations.holds that school success is very much determined by the emotional stability of the child that includes a sense of security and belongingness that is imparted firstly by the parents and then by the impact of other agents of socialization. Studies have linked parenting behaviour and attitudes to children's aggression and other behavioural problems that are found to affect their school performance.

DATA GATHERING PROCEDURE AND STATISTICAL TECHNIQUE USED

Data Collection

The necessary evidence was collected in line with the objectives of the study. All the 220 teenager girls were individually approaches by the researcher. By personal contact, all the respondents were interviewed with the help of the structured schedule developed for the study.

Keeping in view the convenience of the teenager girls, several visits were made for the collection of data during the course of investigation. Every care was taken for maintaining accuracy of implementation and wherever possible suitable cross-checking was done.

During the collection of the data, help from DUDA office Moradabad was taken.

Period of Investigation

The data collection was initiated from December 2007 to December 2008.

Hypotheses

1. Nature, attitude and relationship of girls with her selected mothers.
2. Identity the responsibility and role of teenagers in household activities with working and non-working mothers.
3. Interpersonal relationship teenagers and mothers with reference to sharing experiences in daily life about the friend circle, and personal problems.

Statistical Techniques

The following statistical techniques have been applied in the analysis of data:

Percentage

$$\text{Percentage} = \frac{\text{The sum of all the responses}}{\text{Total number of all the responses}} \times 100$$

Arithmetic Mean

The arithmetic average mean of a variable is obtained by dividing the sum of its given values by their number. If the variable is denoted by X and if n value of X are given X_1, X_2, . . . X_n, then the arithmetic mean of X is

$$\bar{X} = \sum_{i=1}^{n} X_{1/n}$$

Weighted Mean (Scores)

All the items are not of equal importance. At that time they are given proper weights according to their relative importance, and then the average which is calculated on the basis of these weights is called weighted average of the weighted mean:

$$\text{Weighted mean} = \frac{W_1X_1 + W_2X_2 + W_3X_3 + \ldots W_nX_n}{W_1 + W_2 + W_3 \ldots W_n}$$

$$= \frac{\sum wX}{\sum w}$$

Standard Deviation (S.D.)

It is defined as the square root of the means of the squares of the deviations taken from arithmetic mean:

(i) For ungrouped data – S.D. $= \sqrt{1/n\sum(\sum X_i - \bar{X})^2}$

(ii) For grouped data – S.D. $= \sqrt{1/n\sum f_i - (X_i - \bar{X})^2}$

Chi-square Test

In order to test the independence of two attributes a Chi-square test was applied as:

$$\chi^2 = \sum_{i=1}^{n} \frac{(0_i - E_i)^2}{E_i}$$

Where,

O_i = Observed frequency of ith cell

E_i = Expected frequency of ith cell

In rxc contingency table, χ^2 value is compared at (r-1) × (C-1) degrees of freedom with theoretical value of χ^2 at 5 per cent level of significance.

'Z' test

It was applied to test the difference between two sample means and when the observations in two set are independent. Following formula is used:

$$Z = \frac{(\bar{X}_1 - \bar{X}_2)}{\sqrt{\frac{S_1^2}{n_1} + \frac{+S_2^2}{n_2}}}$$

where,

$\bar{X}_1$ = Mean of first sample

X_2 = Mean of second sample

S_1 = Standard deviation of first sample

S_2 = Standard deviation of second sample

n_1 = Number of respondent (in first sample)

n_2 = Number of respondent (in second sample)

Correlation Coefficient

Karl Pearson has given a coefficient of correlation for the measurement of linear relationship, which exists between two variables. If X and Y are two variables and if $E(X,Y) \neq 0$ then correlation coefficient (r) is:

$$r = \frac{\text{Cov.}(X, Y)}{\sqrt{\text{Var.}(X).\ \text{Var.}(Y)}}$$

or

$$= \frac{\Sigma\, xy}{\sqrt{\Sigma x^2 . \Sigma y^2}}$$

where,

$$\Sigma xy = \left[\Sigma XY - \frac{\Sigma X \Sigma Y}{n}\right]$$

$$\Sigma x^2 = \left[\Sigma X^2 - \frac{(\Sigma X)^2}{n}\right]$$

$$\Sigma y^2 = \left[\Sigma Y^2 - \frac{(\Sigma Y)^2}{n}\right]$$

and n = Sample size

Here, one variable is dependent on other. For testing the significance of correlation coefficient (r), t test is applied. Degree of lack of relationship or coefficient of alienation is measured as:

$$K = \sqrt{1 - r^2}$$

FINDINGS AND DISCUSSION

The empirical results and its discussion have been presented in this chapter. For the purpose of convenience. The collected data were categorized, analyzed, tabulated and interpreted as per the objectives of the study. For the purpose of convenience, the findings of the study have been sub-divided under the following heads:-

I. To know the socio-demographic status of teenager girls.

II. To know the nature; attitude and relationship of teenagers with her working and non-working mothers.

III. To identify the responsibility and role of teenagers in household activities with selected mothers.

IV. To understand interpersonal relationship between mothers and girls.

V. Patterns of interaction between mothers and girls.

(a) Sharing of experiences and activities

(b) Knowledge of friends

(c) Discipline maintained of different levels with mothers.

(d) Personal problems.

THE SOCIO-DEMOGRAPHIC STATUS OF TEENAGER GIRLS

Age

Table 5.1: Distribution of teenager girls according to age

Age group (years)	Girls of working mother	Girls of non-working mothers	Total
13 - 14	28 (25.4)	24 (21.8)	52 (23.6)
15 - 16	30 (27.3)	37 (33.6)	67 (30.5)
17 - 18	52 (47.3)	49 (44.6)	101 (45.9)
Total	110 (100.0)	110 (100.0)	220 (100.0)
χ^2	1.128		$P > 0.05$

(Figures in parentheses indicate percentage of respective values).

Table 5.1 shows that distribution of teenager girls according to age, 47.3 per cent girls of working mother belonged to 17 to 18 years age group followed by 27.3 per cent girl respondents of 15 to 16 years age group. 44.6 per cent girls of non-working mother belonged to 17 to 18 years age group followed by 33.6 per cent girls of 15 to 16 years age group. 21.8 per cent girls of non-working mother belonged to 13 to 14 years age group. Teenager period of the children is a crucial time, where mother feels that it is even more important to spend time with their children. The observed value of χ^2 was non-significant at 5 per cent level of significance.

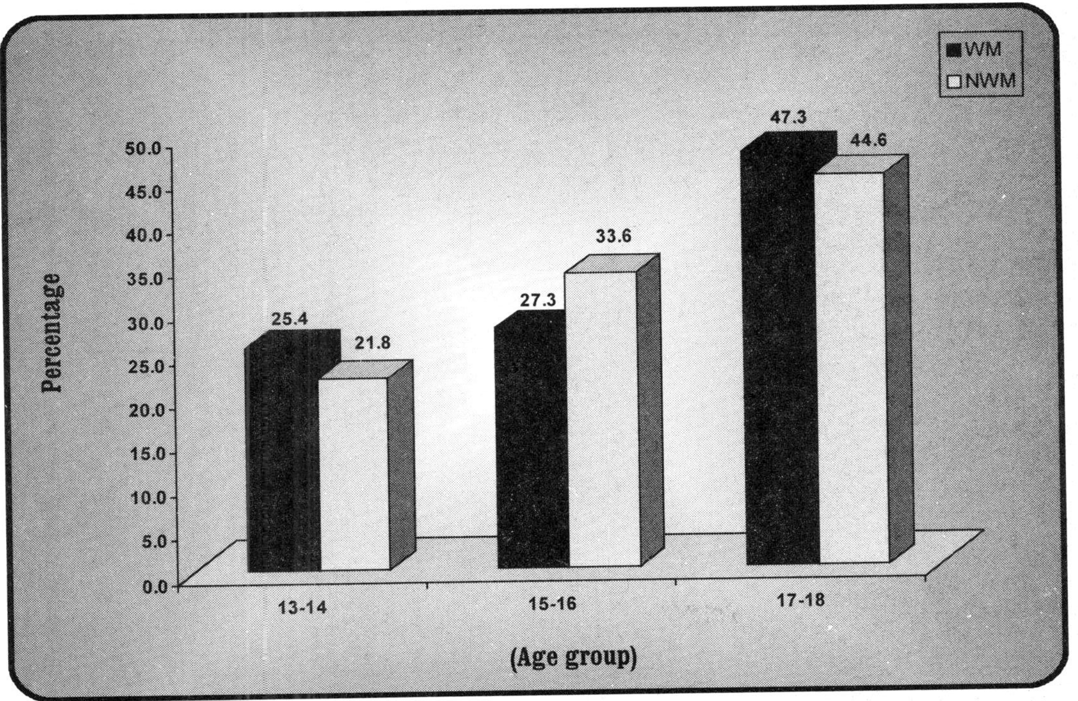

Fig. 5.1: Distribution of teenager girls according to age

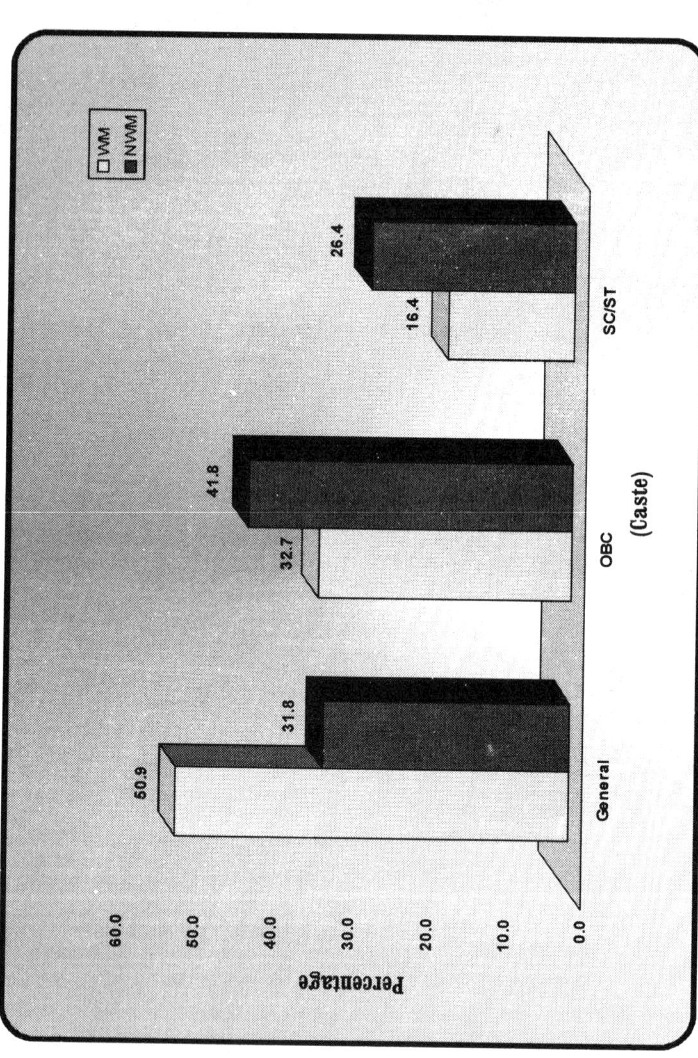

Fig. 5.2: Distribution of teenager girls according to caste

Caste

Table 5.2: Distribution of teenager girls according to caste

Caste	Girls of working mother	Girls of non-working mother	Total
General	56 (50.9)	35 (31.8)	91 (41.4)
OBC	36 (32.7)	46 (41.8)	82 (37.3)
SC/ST	18 (16.4)	29 (26.4)	47 (21.3)
Total	110 (100.0)	110 (100.0)	220 (100.0)
χ^2	8.640*		$P < 0.05$

(Figures in parentheses indicate percentage of respective values).

Table 5.2 reveals that distribution of girl's respondents according to caste, 50.9 per cent girls belonged to general category of working mother whereas 32.7 per cent girls belonged to OBC category. 41.8 per cent girls were belonged to OBC category of non-working mother whereas 31.8 per cent girls were from general category. The employment imposes a substantial stress on the mother as well as on their adolescent daughters. Environment and caste play an important role to interpersonal relationship with working and non-working mothers and girls respondents. The observed value of χ^2 (8.640*) was significant at 5 per cent level of significance.

Religion

It is well illustrated from the above table that religion wise distribution of teenager girls, 77.7 per cent girls were belonged to Hindu family, whereas 6.8 per cent girls from Muslim family. 8.7 per cent girls were from Sikh religion and only 6.8 per cent girls were from Christian family. The observed value of χ^2 (2.147) was non-significant at 5 per cent level of significance.

Table 5.3 Distribution of teenager girls according to religion

Religion	Girls of working mother	Girls of non-working mothers	Total
General	90 (81.8)	81 (73.6)	171 (77.7)
Muslim	6 (5.4)	9 (8.2)	15 (6.8)
Sikh	8 (7.4)	11 (10.0)	19 (8.7)
Christian	6 (5.4)	9 (8.2)	15 (6.8)
Total	110 (100.0)	110 (100.0)	220 (100.0)
χ^2	2.147		P > 0.05

(Figures in parentheses indicate percentage of respective values).

Family type

Table 5.4 Distribution of teenager girls according to family type

Family type	Girls of working mother	Girls of non-working mothers	Total
Nuclear	75 (68.2)	59 (53.6)	134 (60.9)
Joint	35 (31.8)	51 (46.4)	86 (39.1)
Total	110 (100.0)	110 (100.0)	220 (100.0)
χ^2	4.887*		P < 0.05

(Figures in parentheses indicate percentage of respective values).

It is clear from Table 5.4 that distribution of teenager girls according to family type, 68.2 per cent girls working mother were belonged to nuclear family and 31.8 per cent girls from joint family system. 53.6 per cent girls of non-working mothers were belonged to nuclear family whereas 46.4 per cent girls were from joint family. Family type also plays a crucial role in relationship of mothers and teenaged girls. The calculated value of χ^2 (4.887*) was significant at 5.0 per cent level of significance at 1 d.f.

Family size

Table 5.5 Distribution of teenager girls according to family size

Family size	Girls of working mother	Girls of non-working mothers	Total
2 to 4 members	58 (52.7)	31 (28.2)	89 (40.5)
5 to 7 members	33 (30.0)	37 (33.6)	70 (31.8)
8 and above	19 (17.3)	42 (38.2)	61 (27.7)
Total	110 (100.0)	110 (100.0)	220 (100.0)
χ^2	17.092*	$P < 0.05$	

(Figures in parentheses indicate percentage of respective values).

Table 5.5 shows that distribution of teenager girls according to family size, 52.7 per cent girls of working mother have 2 to 4 members family size whereas 30.0 per cent girls have 5 to 7 members in family. 38.2 per cent girls of non-working mothers have 8 and above family size whereas 33.6 per cent girls of non-working mother have 5 to 7 members in family. Full time homemakers, employed mothers differentiate less between sons and daughters in their discipline style and in their goals for their children. Family size is not alone responsible for the kind of relationships that develop among family members. Instead, they depend upon a number of factors, four of which are especially important. The observed value of χ^2 (17.092*) was significant at 5.0 per cent, 2 d.f.

The larger the family, the greater the number of interactional systems and, normally, the greater the friction in the home, however, friction is often counteracted by the authoritarian discipline of the parents. To avoid the unhealthy home climate that friction gives rise to and to enable each family member to live in harmony with other family members. Parents of large families more often use authoritarian child training methods than do parents of smaller ones.

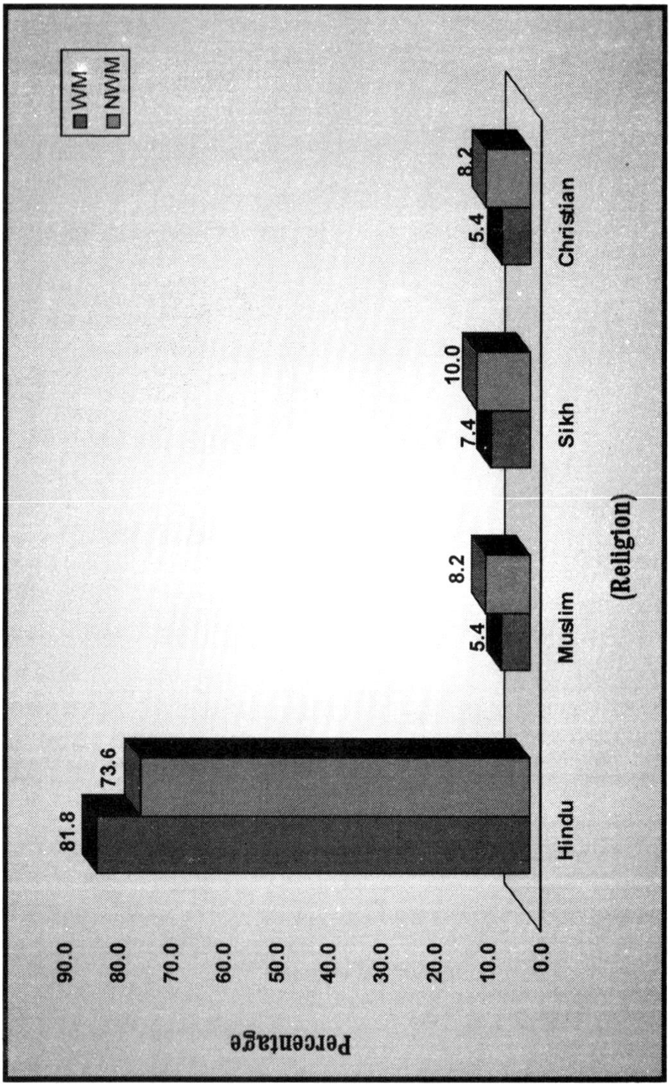

Fig. 5.3: Distribution of teenager girls according to religion

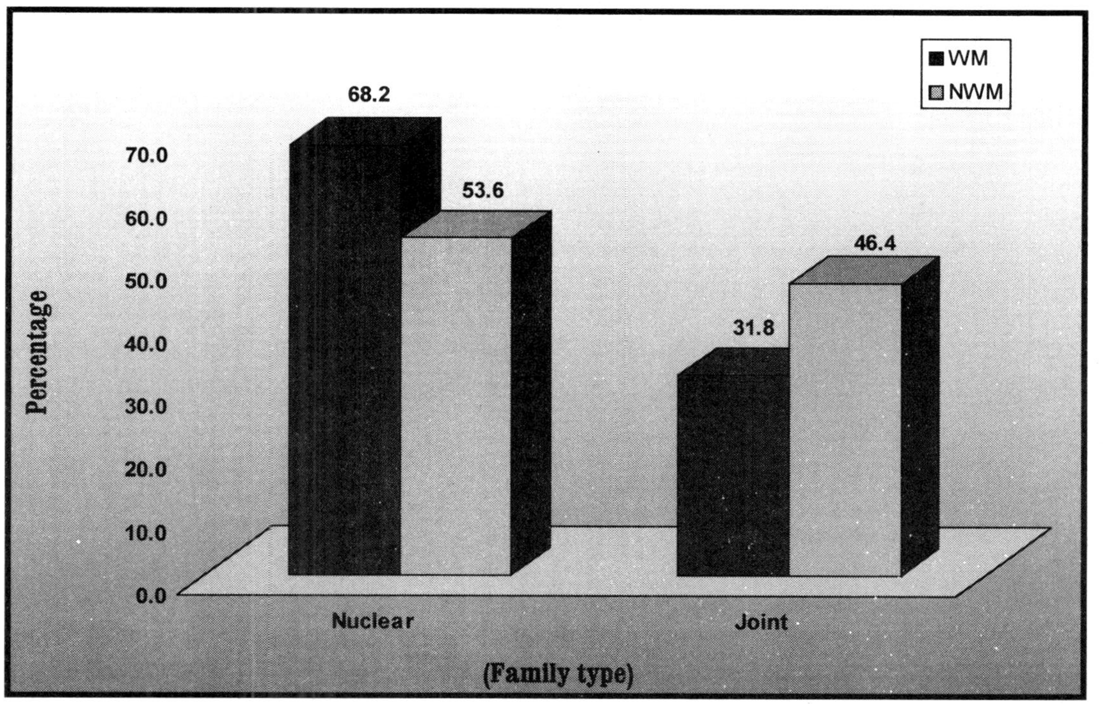

Fig. 5.4: Distribution of teenager girls according to family type

Economic status

Table 5.6: Distribution of teenager girls according to economic status

Economic status	Girls of working mother	Girls of non-working mothers	Total
Lower	29 (26.4)	47 (42.7)	76 (34.5)
Middle	52 (47.2)	45 (40.9)	97 (44.1)
Higher	29 (26.4)	18 (16.4)	47 (21.4)
Total	110 (100.0)	110 (100.0)	220 (100.0)
χ^2	7.343*	P < 0.05	

Table 5.6 reveals that distribution of teenager girls according to economic status, 47.2 per cent girls of working mother have middle economic status while 26.4 per cent girls have lower and higher economic status. 42.7 per cent girls of non-working mother have lower economic status whereas 40.9 per cent girls have middle economic status. There is much impact of economic status on the relations of mother and teenager girls, because in all the disputes, money plays an important role. Healthy relations are established in high status families. The observed value of χ^2 (7.343*) was significant at 5.0 per cent, 2 d.f.

Income

Table 5.7: Distribution of working women according to income

Income of working women	Frequency	Per cent
Up to Rs. 5000	45	40.9
Rs. 5000 to Rs. 10000	29	26.4
Rs. 10000 to Rs. 15000	25	22.7
Rs. 15000 and above	11	10.0
Total	110	100.00

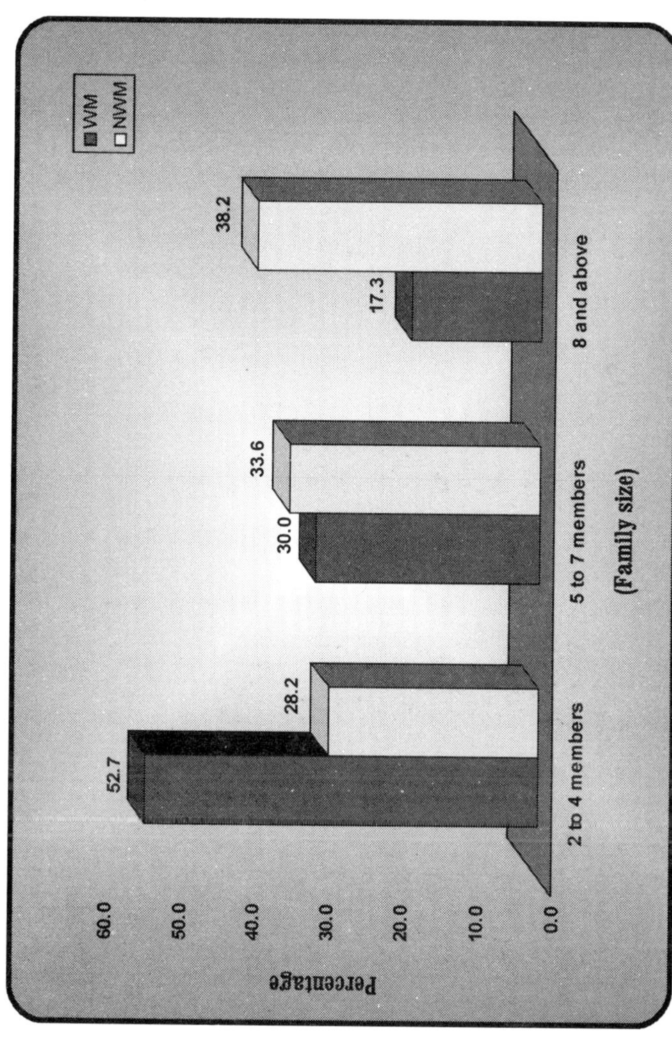

Fig. 5.5: Distribution of teenager girls according to family size

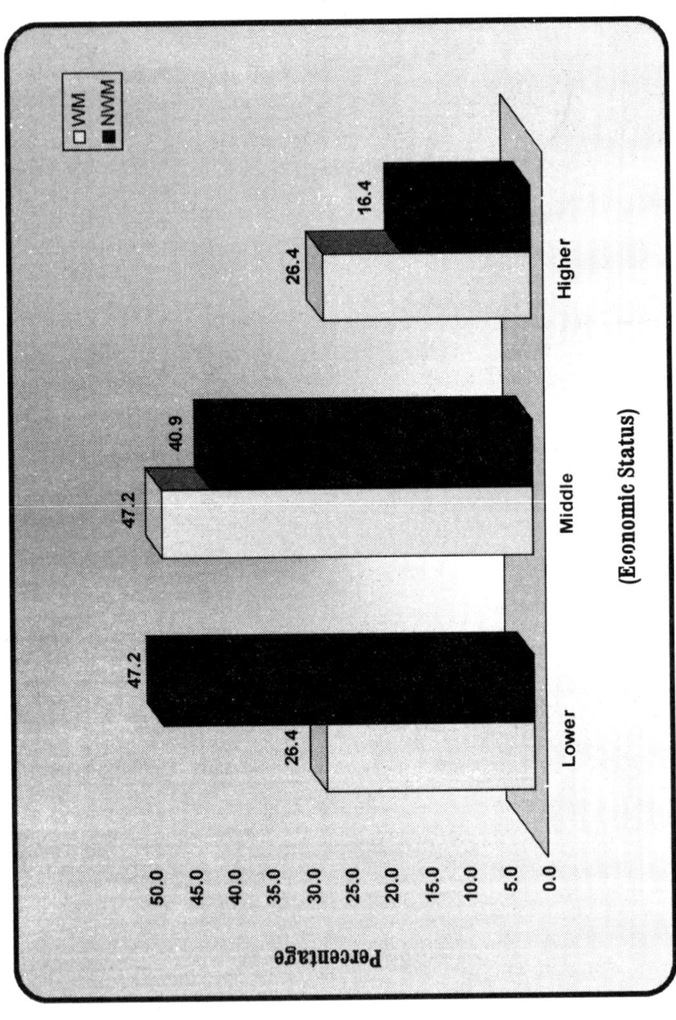

Fig. 5.6: Distribution of teenager girls according to economic status

Table 5.7 illustrated that distribution of women according to income, 40.9 per cent women have earned up to Rs. 5,000 monthly, 26.4 per cent women have earned Rs. 5,000 to Rs. 10,000 monthly and 22.7 per cent working women earned Rs. 10,000 to Rs. 15,000 monthly. Indian society and people are prejudiced against the employment of mothers with young children. The employment of housewives outside their homes has got an adverse effect on the performance of their children in study particularly their adolescent, who have to attend the household jobs like preparation of meals, cleaning of house, care of siblings, washing clothes etc. which are normally attended by the housewives.

Table 5.8 Distribution of girls according to family income

Family size	Girls of working mother	Girls of non-working mother	Total
Up to Rs. 10,000	30 (27.3)	36 (32.7)	66 (30.0)
Rs. 10,000 to 20,000	32 (29.1)	48 (43.6)	80 (36.4)
Rs. 20,000 to Rs. 30,000	38 (34.5)	20 (18.2)	58 (26.4)
Rs. 30,000 and above	10 (9.1)	6 (5.5)	16 (7.2)
Total	110 (100.0)	110 (100.0)	220 (100.0)
χ^2	10.332*	$P < 0.05$	

(Figures in parentheses indicate percentage of respective values).

Table 5.8 shows that distribution of girls according to family monthly income, 34.5 per cent girls of working women have family monthly income Rs. 20,000 to Rs. 30,000 whereas 29.1 per cent girls of working women have family income Rs. 10,000 to Rs. 20,000. 43.6 per cent girls of non-working women have monthly family income Rs. 10,000 to Rs. 20,000 followed by 32.7 per cent were up to Rs. 10,000. 9.1 per cent girls of working women have family income Rs. 30,000 and above whereas 5.5 per cent girls of non-working women. The calculated value of χ^2 (10.332*) was significant at 5.0 per cent level of significance.

THE NATURE, ATTITUDE AND RELATIONSHIP OF TEENAGERS' WITH HER WORKING AND NON-WORKING MOTHERS

Several investigators have reported that youngsters and adolescents perceive their mothers as being more nurturant – more actively concerned about their offspring's development and well-being than their fathers. Both male and female adolescents reported that their mothers exert more influence than their fathers, reflecting perhaps the greater role of the mother in the child rearing process. On the other hand, findings indicate that females, as compared with males, more often report receiving praise and affection from their fathers.

Table 5.9 Relationship of daughter of working and non-working mother with her parents according to their age

Age group (years)	Daughter of working mother			Daughter of non-working mother		
	N	Mean score	S.D.	N	Mean score	S.D.
13 - 14	28	0.88	0.12	24	0.86	0.11
15 - 16	30	0.89	0.11	37	0.81	0.09
17 - 18	52	0.80	0.14	49	0.79	0.13
Total	110	0.85	0.13	110	0.82	0.12
Z	0.8280*			P > 0.05		

Table 5.9 shows relationship of daughter of working and non-working mothers with her parents according to their age group. It is more in age group of 15-16 years of working mother having mean score 0.89, whereas this relationship is least in age group 17-18 years having mean score of 0.80. In non-working mother daughter the relationship is more and good in age group 13-14 years with mean score (0.86) followed by age

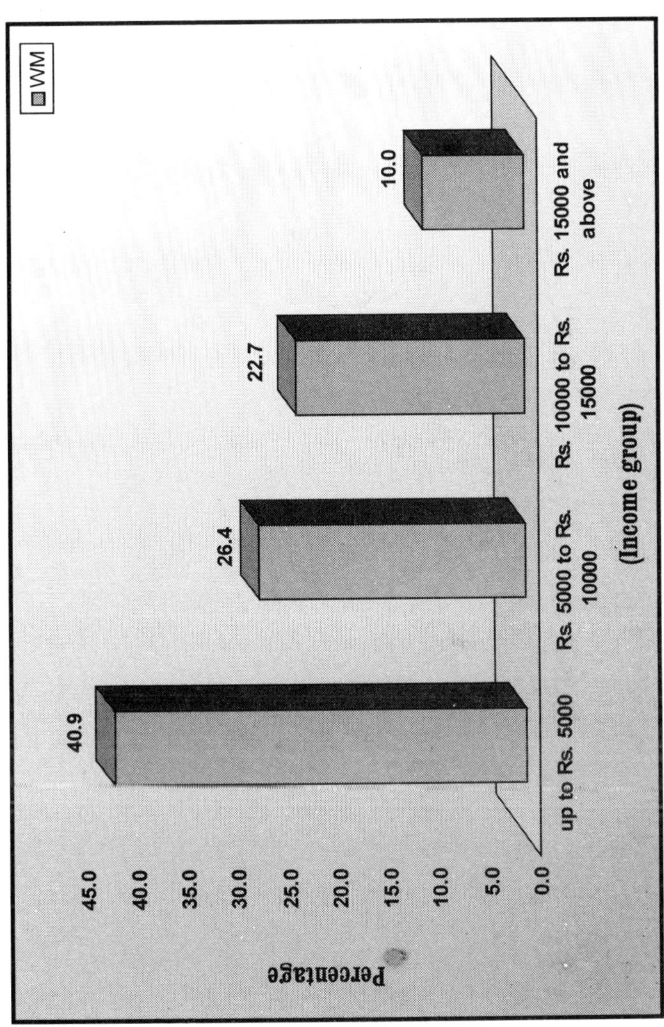

Fig. 5.7: Distribution of working women according to Income

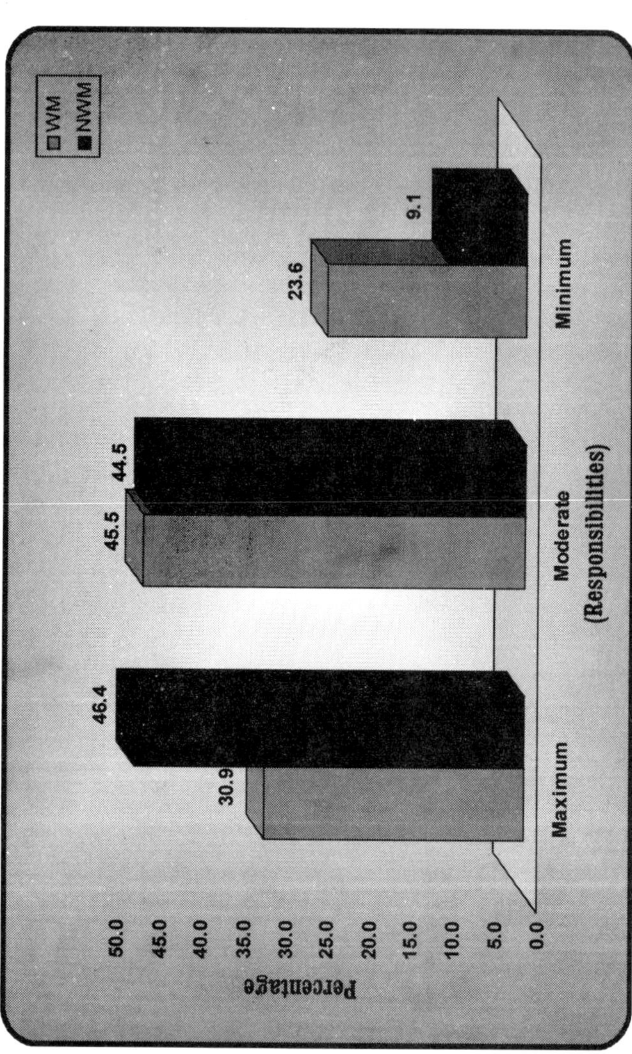

Fig. 5.8: Distribution according to the responsibilities of household on both working and non-working mothers

group 15-16 years with mean score 0.81, whereas, this relationship is least in age group 17-18 years having mean score of 0.79. Children of mothers who enjoy their work and remain committed to parenting show very favourable adjustment – a higher sense of self-esteem, more positive family and peer relations, less gender – stereotyped beliefs, and better grades in school. Girls, especially, profit from the image of female competence. African-American adolescent girls whose mothers worked during the daughter's early years are more likely to stay in school. Overall, daughters of employed mothers perceive the woman's role as involving more freedom of choice and satisfaction and are more ambitious and career oriented. These benefits undoubtedly result from parenting practices. Employed mothers who value their parenting role are more likely to use authoritative child rearing and co-regulation – granting their child independence with oversight. Also, children in dual earner households devote more daily hours to doing homework under parental guidance and participate more in household chores. And maternal employment results in more time with fathers, who take on greater child-care responsibility. More paternal contact is related to higher intelligence and achievement, mature social behaviour, and gender stereotype flexibility. However, when employment places heavy demands on the mother's schedule, children are at risk for ineffective parenting, working long hours and spending little time with children are associated with less favourable adjustment. In contrast, part-time employment seems to have benefits for children of all ages, probably because it prevents work overload, thereby helping mothers meet children's needs in dual-earner families, the husband's willingness to share responsibilities help mothers engage in effective parenting. If the father helps very little or not at all, the mother carries a double load, at home and at work, leading to fatigue, distress, and reduced time and energy for children.

Employed mothers and dual-earner parents need assistance from work settings and communities in their child-rearing roles. Part-time employment, flexible schedules, job-sharing, and paid leave when children are ill-help parents juggle the demands of work and child rearing. Although these supports are available in other industrialized nations, at present only unpaid employment leave is mandated. Equal pay and equal employment opportunities for women also are important. Because these policies enhance financial status and morale, they improve the way mothers feel and behave when they arrive home at the end of the working day. The observed value of Z (0.8280) was non-significant at 5.0 per cent level of significance.

Table 5.10 Relationship of daughter of working and non-working mother with her peers according to age group

Age group (years)	Daughter of working mother			Daughter of non-working mother		
	N	Mean score	S.D.	N	Mean score	S.D.
13-14	28	0.68	0.19	24	0.85	0.09
15-16	30	0.91	0.15	37	0.73	0.13
17-18	52	0.83	0.17	49	0.71	0.16
Total	110	0.82	0.18	110	0.72	0.14
Z		2.348*			P < 0.05	

It is very much clear from Table 5.10 that daughters of working mother's have good and better relationship with their peers according to their age group in age group 15-16 as its mean score is 0.91 whereas, this relationship is least in age group 13-14 years having mean score of 0.68 and standard deviation 0.19. Relationship of daughters of non-working mothers with her peers according to their age is more in age group 13-14 years with mean score 0.85 whereas, it is least in age group 17-18 years having an mean score of 0.71 and S.D. 0.16. Teenager girls having good relations with family members continue to have same with their peer group. This is because of family background, which leaves indelible imprint on their children. This continues further and children behave in the same way with group also. The calculated value of Z (2.348*) was significant at 5.0 level of significance hence there was significant difference between relationship of working and non-working mother's daughter with her peers.

Table 5.11 Responsibility of household on daughter of working and non-working mother according to age group

Age group (years)	Daughter of working mother			Daughter of non-working mother		
	N	Mean score	S.D.	N	Mean score	S.D.
13-14	28	0.81	0.18	24	0.91	0.18
15-16	30	0.89	0.17	37	0.87	0.16
17-18	52	0.79	0.15	49	0.88	0.17
Total	110	0.82	0.16	110	0.89	0.17
Z		3.1448*			P < 0.05	

It is well illustrated from Table 5.11 that responsibility of household on daughter of working mother according to age group is more in age group 15-16 years having mean score of 0.89 and S.D. 0.17 whereas, it is least in age group of 17-18 years having mean score 0.79 and standard deviation 0.15. Responsibility of household on daughters of non-working mothers according to their age group is more in age group of 13-14 years having mean score 0.91 whereas, this responsibility is least in age group 15-16 (0.87) and 17-18 years having mean score 0.88 and standard deviation (0.17). The calculated value of Z (3.1448*) was significant at 5.0 per cent level of significance conclude that responsibility of household on working and non-working mother's daughter have significant difference.

Table 5.12 shows that interaction between working mother and their daughters according to age group is more in 13-14 years having mean score 0.90 whereas, this interaction is less in age group 17-18 years (0.77) and S.D. (0.20). Interaction between non-working mother and their daughter according to age group is more in age group 13-14 years having mean score (0.91) and these have positive interaction with their mother whereas it is least in age group 17-18 years having mean score

(0.75) which shows that they do not have good and positive interaction with their mothers. The calculated value of Z (1.0568) was non-significant at 5.0 per cent level.

Table 5.12 Interaction between working and non-working mothers and their daughters according to age group

Age group (years)	Daughter of working mother			Daughter of non-working mother		
	N	Mean score	S.D.	N	Mean score	S.D.
13-14	28	0.90	0.11	24	0.91	0.12
15-16	30	0.82	0.10	37	0.83	0.11
17-18	52	0.77	0.20	49	0.75	0.17
Total	110	0.80	0.13	110	0.78	0.15
Z	1.0568			$P < 0.05$		

Table 5.13 Career aspiration of daughters of working and non-working mothers according to their age

Age group (years)	Daughter of working mother			Daughter of non-working mother		
	N	Mean score	S.D.	N	Mean score	S.D.
13-14	28	0.90	0.05	24	0.82	0.07
15-16	30	0.87	0.07	37	0.91	0.12
17-18	52	0.86	0.09	49	0.87	0.10
Total	110	0.88	0.06	110	0.85	0.90
Z	0.3488			$P > 0.05$		

Table 5.13 shows that career aspiration of daughters of working mothers in accordance to their age is more in age group 13-14 years having mean score of 0.90 whereas, this career aspiration is least in age group 17-18 years having mean score of 0.86 and S.D. (0.09). It is very much clear from the above Table that the daughters of non-working mother are more conscious about their career in the age group 15-16 years having

a mean score of 0.91 whereas, the career aspiration is least in the age group 13-14 years having a mean score of 0.82 and S.D. 0.07. Educated and working mother have an important role is selecting career line for teenager girls, which is not possible with non-working mother. Because level of thinking of an educated and working mother is entirely different from non-working and uneducated mother. They are supposed to be more conscious about the career of her daughter. The calculated value of Z (0.3488) was non-significant at 5.0 per cent level of significance hence, career aspiration of daughters' shows significant difference.

Table 5.14 Sharing of experiences and activities between working and non-working mothers and their daughters according to age

Age group (years)	Daughter of working mother			Daughter of non-working mother		
	N	Mean score	S.D.	N	Mean score	S.D.
13 - 14	28	0.83	0.12	24	0.70	0.10
15 - 16	30	0.76	0.18	37	0.80	0.20
17 - 18	52	0.63	0.22	49	0.61	0.24
Total	110	0.77	0.16	110	0.71	0.18
Z	2.6130*			$P < 0.05$		

Table 5.14 reveals that sharing of experiences and activities between working mothers and their daughters according to their age group is more in age group 13-14 years having mean (0.83) whereas it is least with age group 17-18 years having mean score of 0.63 and S.D. 0.22. Sharing of experiences and activities between non-working mother and their daughter according to their age group is more in age group 15-16 years having an mean score of 0.80 whereas, this sharing of experiences is least in age group 17-18 years having an mean scores of 0.61 and S.D. 0.24. The observed value of Z (2.6130*) was significant at 5 per cent level of significance, sharing of experiences and activities shows significant differences.

Table 5.15 Knowledge of friends of daughters of working and non-working mothers according to age

Age group (years)	Daughter of working mother			Daughter of non-working mother		
	N	Mean score	S.D.	N	Mean score	S.D.
13-14	28	0.88	0.21	24	0.79	0.11
15-16	30	0.84	0.20	37	0.85	0.19
17-18	52	0.76	0.31	49	0.74	0.23
Total	110	0.83	0.24	110	0.80	0.20
Z		1.0071			P > 0.05	

The above Table 5.15 shows that knowledge of friends of daughters of working mothers is more in age group 13-14 years having mean score of 0.88 whereas it is least with age group 17-18 years having mean score of 0.76 and S.D. 0.31. The above Table further shows that knowledge of friends of daughters to their non-working mother with respect to their age is more in age group 15-16 years (0.85) whereas it is least in age group 17-14 years having an mean score of 0.74 and standard deviation (0.23). Working mothers are aware about the friends of her teenager daughter. They seem to be afraid of her daughter about indulgence is bad activities. Puberty age is more sensitive. At this stage, mothers used to have an eye on her daughter's activities like, while taking on telephone, writing letter to friends, checking her room, know the status of friends, her friend's family background, about class studies etc. The calculated value of 'Z' was non-significant at 5.0 per cent level of significance.

It is well illustrated from Table 5.16 that discipline of daughters of working mothers according to their age is more in age group 15-16 years having mean scores of 0.88 whereas discipline of daughters is least in age group 17-18 years with a mean score of 0.78 and S.D. (0.18). It is well illustrated from Table 5.16 that discipline of daughters by their non-working mother with respect to their age group is more in age group 15-16 years having mean score of 0.83 whereas it is least in age group 17-18 years having mean score of 0.74. The observed value of Z (3.294*) is significant at 5.0 per cent level of significance.

Table 5.16 Discipline of daughters of working and non-working mothers with respect to their age group

Age group (years)	Daughter of working mother			Daughter of non-working mother		
	N	Mean score	S.D.	N	Mean score	S.D.
13-14	28	0.81	0.12	24	0.78	0.12
15-16	30	0.88	0.14	37	0.83	0.16
17-18	52	0.78	0.18	49	0.74	0.14
Total	110	0.83	0.13	110	0.77	0.14
Z	3.294*			P < 0.05		

TO IDENTIFY THE RESPONSIBILITY AND ROLE OF TEENAGERS IN HOUSEHOLD ACTIVITIES WITH SELECTED MOTHERS

Table 5.17 Frequency distribution according to the responsibility of household on both working and non-working mothers

A Responsibility	Working mothers		Non-working mothers	
	Frequency	Percentage	Frequency	Percentage
Maximum	34	30.9	51	46.4
Moderate	50	45.5	49	44.5
Minimum	26	23.6	10	9.1
Total	110	100.0	110	100.0
χ^2	10.521*		P < 0.05	

Table 5.17 reveals that 46.4 per cent non-working mothers had greater amount of household responsibilities whereas the

remaining 44.5 per cent the non-working mothers had moderate amount of household responsibilities. On the contrast, 30.9 per cent working mothers revealed that they had high amount of household responsibilities and greater majority of about 45.5 per cent working mothers has moderate amount of household responsibility while the remaining 23.6 per cent the working mother showed that they had very less or few household responsibility.

About 23.6 per cent working mothers have very less or few household responsibilities may be due to the assistance provided by family members or may be due to the paid servants. "Family" of which they themselves teenager a vital part. The overall responsibility of accomplishing the myriad household jobs falls on the shoulder of the housewives. The employment imposes a substantial stress on the home makers as well as on their adolescent daughter. The employment of housewives outside their homes has got an adverse effect on the performance of their children in study particularly their adolescent daughters, who have to attend the households job like preparation of meals, cleaning of house, dish washing, washing of clothes, ironing of clothes and care of siblings which are normally attended by the housewives. The observed value of χ^2 (10.521*) was significant at 5.0 per cent level of significance.

Table 5.18 shows that 73.6 per cent non-working mothers have a very good, healthy and positive interaction with their daughters whereas 14.5 per cent non-working mothers have moderate amount of interaction with their daughter and the remaining 11.9 per cent non-working mothers have least amount of interaction with their daughters. On the other hand, 47.3 per cent working mothers have a good positive interaction with their daughters, whereas 41.8 per cent working mothers have moderate amount of interaction with their daughters and the remaining 10.9 per cent working mothers have least amount of interaction with their daughters.

Table 5.18 Frequency distribution of patterns of interaction between mother and daughters of both working and non-working mothers

B Responsibility	Working mothers		Non-working mothers	
	Frequency	Percentage	Frequency	Percentage
Positive	52	47.3	81	73.6
Moderate	46	41.8	16	14.5
Least	12	10.9	13	11.9
Total	110	100.0	110	100.0
χ^2	20.879*		$P < 0.05$	

The observed value of χ^2 is 20.879* which is significant at 5.0 per cent level of significance.

Table 5.19 Frequency distribution of sharing of experiences and activities between mother and daughters

B1 Responsibility	Working mothers		Non-working mothers	
	Frequency	Percentage	Frequency	Percentage
High	45	40.9	50	45.5
Medium	34	30.9	42	38.2
Low	31	28.2	18	16.3
Total	110	100.0	110	100.0
χ^2	4.554		$P > 0.05$	

Table 5.19 shows that 45.5 per cent non-working mothers have very good understanding with their daughters and they share their experiences and problem with one another and have a friendly relationship with one another whereas 38.2 per cent non-working mothers have moderate amount of understanding with their daughters and the remaining 16.3 per cent non-working mothers have very less understanding with their daughters and they do not share their experience and problems with one another.

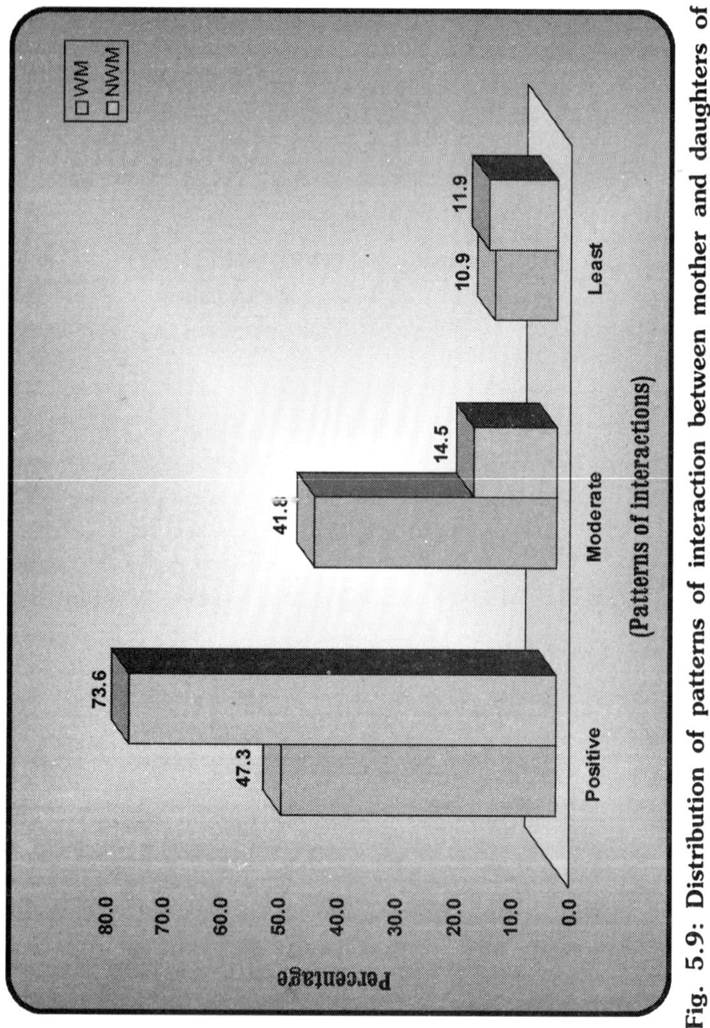

Fig. 5.9: Distribution of patterns of interaction between mother and daughters of both working and non-working mothers

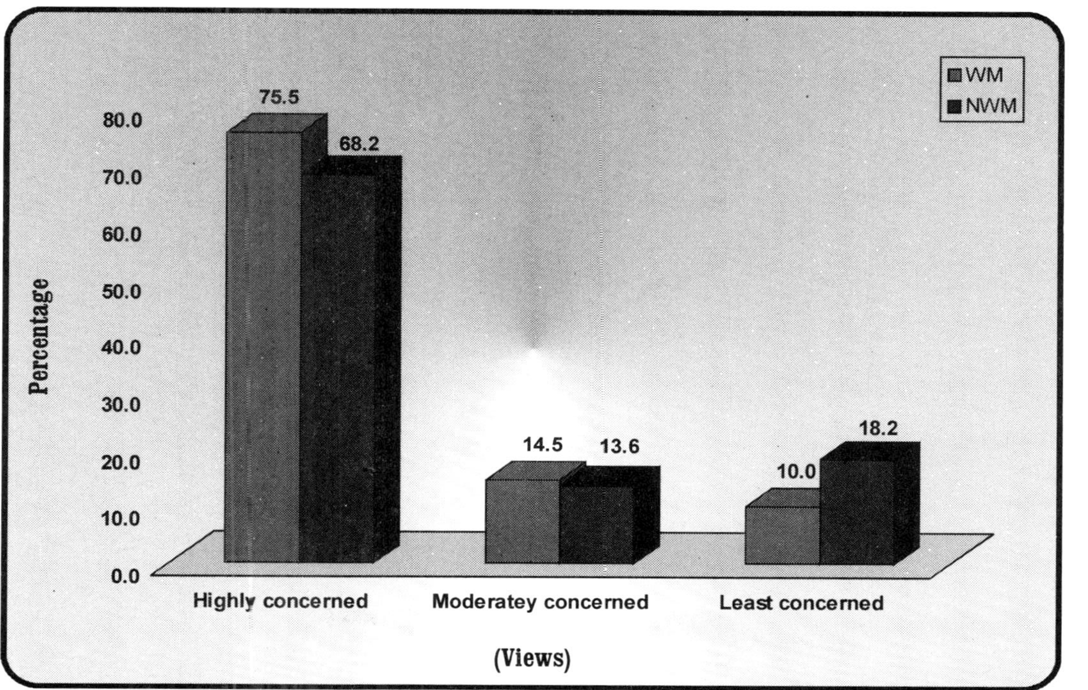

Fig. 5.10: Distribution of mothers view regarding daughters career

On the other side, 40.9 per cent working mothers have good understanding with their daughters and they have a friendly relationship with one another whereas 30.9 per cent working mothers have moderate amount of understanding with their daughters and about 28.2 per cent working mothers have less understanding with their daughters and they do not share their experiences and problems with one another, which is quite high in comparison to the non-working mothers.

Table 5.20 Frequency distribution of mothers awareness and views regarding her daughters friends

B2 Respon-sibility	Working mothers		Non-working mothers	
	Frequency	Percentage	Frequency	Percentage
Good	72	65.5	64	58.2
Average	35	31.8	32	29.1
Poor	3	2.7	14	12.7
Total	110	100.0	110	100.0
χ^2	7.723*		P < 0.05	

Table 5.20 shows that the way 58.2 per cent non-working mothers have brought up their daughters very good and they are satisfied with it whereas, 31.8 per cent non-working mothers are falling into the moderate category and about 2.7 per cent non-working mothers are not satisfied the manner they have brought up their daughters.

On the other side, 65.5 per cent working mothers are highly satisfied by their parenting style whereas 31.8 per cent working mothers are falling into the moderate category. The observed value of χ^2 (7.723*) was significant at 5.0 per cent, 2 d.f..

Table 5.21 shows that about 68.2 per cent non-working mothers are highly concerned about their daughters' career and would like their daughters to take up some career and would support them. 13.6 per cent non-working mothers are falling into the moderate category and the remaining 18.2 per cent non-working mothers are least concerned about their daughters' career.

Table 5.21 Frequency distribution of mothers view regarding daughters career

View	Working mothers		Non-working mothers	
	Frequency	Percentage	Frequency	Percentage
Highly concerned	83	75.5	75	68.2
Moderately concerned	16	14.5	15	13.6
Least concerned	11	10.0	20	18.2
Total	110	100.0	110	100.0
χ^2	0.470		P > 0.05	

75.5 per cent working mothers are highly concerned about their daughter's career whereas, 14.5 per cent working mothers are falling into the moderate category. The calculated value of χ^2 (0.470) was non-significant at 5.0 per cent level of significance.

Table 5.22 Frequency distribution of relationship of adolescent girls with her parents

A Responsibility	Non-working mothers' daughters		Working mothers' daughters	
	Frequency	Percentage	Frequency	Percentage
Good	74	67..3	62	56.4
Average	22	20.0	32	29.1
Poor	14	12.7	16	14.5
Total	110	100.0	110	100.0
χ^2	3.044		P > 0.05	

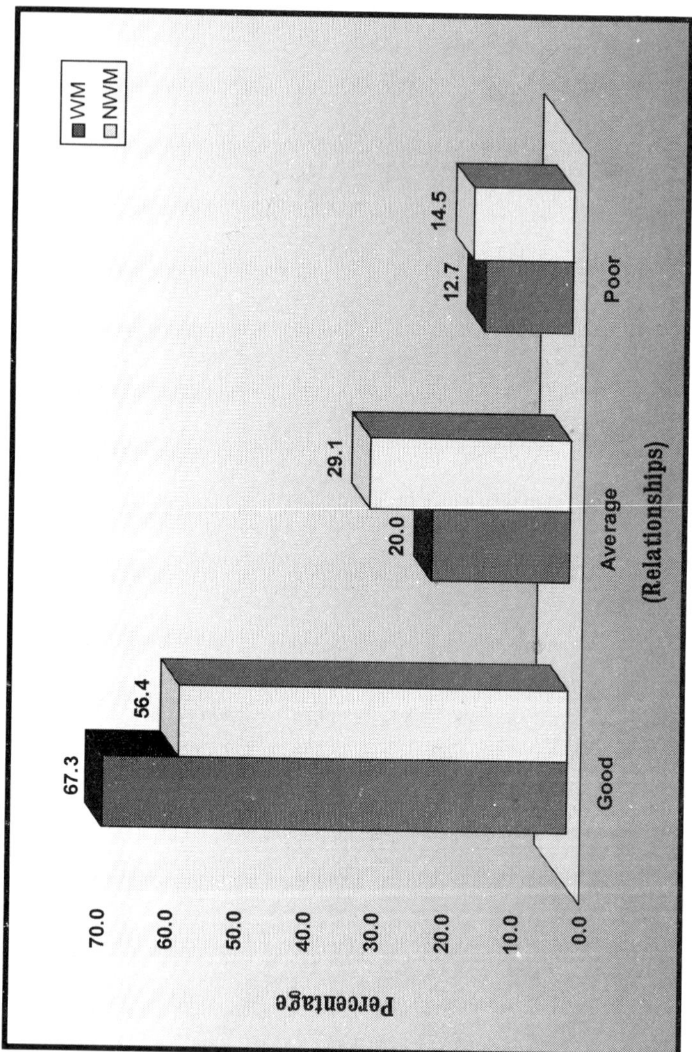

Fig. 5.11: Distribution of relationship of adolescent girl with her parents

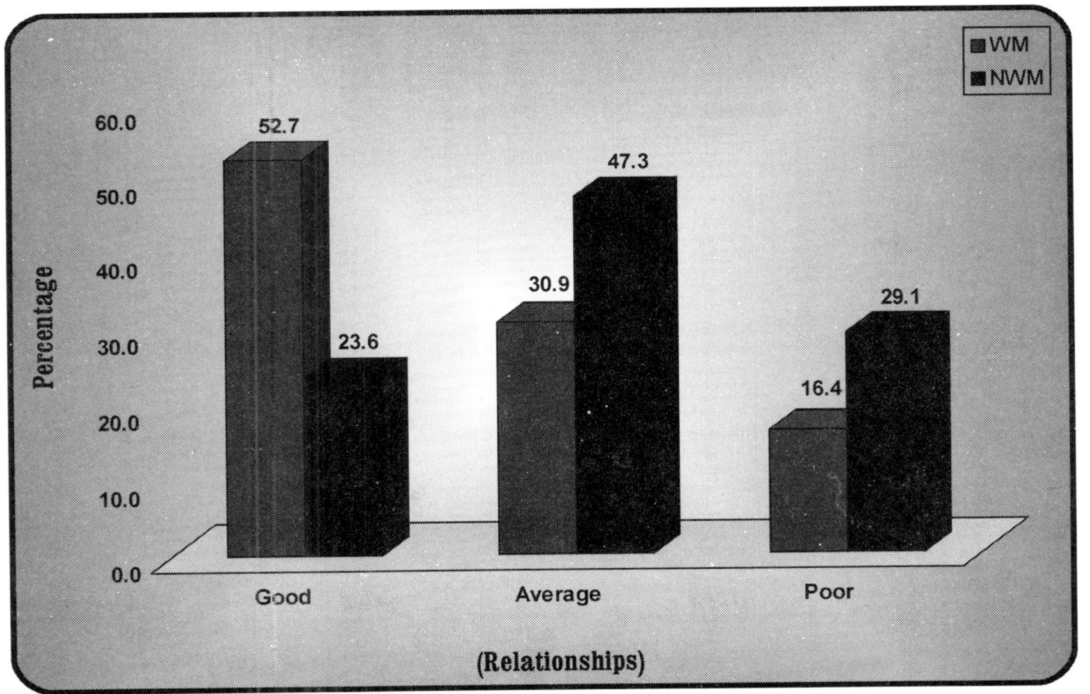

Fig. 5.12: Distribution of adolescent girl with her peers

Table 5.22 shows that 56.4 per cent daughters of non-working mothers share or possess good relationship with their parents whereas 29.1 per cent daughters of non-working mothers are falling into the moderate category and 14.5 per cent daughters of non-working mothers does not share a good relationship with their parents.

On the contrast, 67.3 per cent daughters of working mothers possess good relationship with their parents. 20.0 per cent daughters of working mothers are falling into the moderate category and 12.7 per cent daughters of working mothers does not share a good relationship with their parents. Probably the best and most valued mother-daughter relationship is the kind of friendship. Such friendship based interactions between a mother and her daughter is less susceptible to tension and misunderstanding and there will be a lot of room for dialog rather than that of rushing to enforce authority. Both parties share their secrets freely between themselves and girls raised with such an interaction with their mothers tend to grow up to be confident and strong willed.

A relationship and interaction between a mother and a daughter that tilts favourably towards sisterhood will comprise some of the qualities that are to be found in the friendship kind while also adding characteristics that are unique to sisterhood. Although the bond between a mother and a daughter is not manifested as strongly as in the friendship kind of relationship, without losing touch of the warmth of love to each other they may indeed add competitiveness into the relationship. Any sisterly relationship is characterized by rivalry and competitiveness. That is not a negative thing altogether. In fact, it is positive in that the mother and daughter are idolizing each other so much they want to copy each other. And that competition to outpace the other creates the needed stamina to really know each other better.

The observed value of χ^2 is 3.044 is non-significant at 5.0 per cent level of significance.

Table 5.23 Frequency distribution of adolescent girl with her peers

Relationship	Working mothers' daughters		Non-working mothers' daughters	
	Frequency	Percentage	Frequency	Percentage
Good	58	52.7	26	23.6
Average	34	30.9	52	47.3
Poor	18	16.4	32	29.1
Total	110	100.0	110	100.0
χ^2	19.878*		P < 0.05	

It is clear from the above Table 5.23 that about 47.3 per cent daughters of non-working mothers have average relationship with their peers while 52.7 per cent daughters of working mothers share good relationship with their peers and around 29.1 per cent daughters of non-working mothers do not share good relationship with their peers while on the other side only 16.4 per cent daughters are falling into this category.

The observed value of χ^2 is 19.878* is significant at 5.0 per cent level of significance.

Table 5.24 Frequency distribution of responsibility of household on daughters of working and non-working mothers

Responsibility	Working mothers' daughters		Non-working mothers' daughters	
	Frequency	Percentage	Frequency	Percentage
More	60	54.5	80	72.7
Moderate	32	29.1	18	16.4
Least	18	16.4	12	10.9
Total	110	100.0	110	100.0
χ^2	7.977*		P < 0.05	

The results of Table 5.24 depicts that about 72.7 per cent daughters of non-working mothers feel that they have maximum responsibilities of household upon them and only 10.9 per cent daughters feel that they have least responsibilities and 54.5 per cent daughters of working mothers feel they have maximum responsibilities and only 16.4 per cent daughters feel that they have least responsibilities. Adolescence is a crucial period for healthy development in both psychological and physical terms. During this period attitudes beliefs and values tend to settle into a pattern, out of which emerges the shape and direction of one's lifestyle. For rural India, a girl's adolescence can best be defined as the period of engaging extensively in household activities, as a pre-requisite for a good woman in future, and also the premature end of education. In rural areas there is marginalization of girl child's work and feminization of her labour. Girls are often confined to do household work. The domestic burden of girl child is always higher than the male child. The bulk of rural girl children indirectly contributes to the family purse by taking care of the younger siblings, cleaning utensils, fetching water, collecting fuel and fodder and looking after domestic animals. They also assist in certain agricultural operations such as sowing, weeding, warming, etc. The observed value of χ^2 (7.977*) is significant at 5.0 per cent level of significance.

Table 5.25 Frequency distribution of patterns of interaction between daughters and their working and non-working mothers

Interaction	Working mothers' daughters		Non-working mothers' daughters	
	Frequency	Percentage	Frequency	Percentage
Positive	44	40.0	38	34.5
Moderate	45	40.9	54	49.1
Negative	21	19.1	18	16.4
Total	110	100.0	110	100.0
χ^2	1.488		$P > 0.05$	

Table 5.25 reveals that 34.5 per cent daughters of non-working mothers have a positive and healthy interaction with their mothers whereas 49.1 per cent daughters of non-working mothers are falling into the moderate category whereas, 16.4 per cent daughters of non-working mothers don't have positive interaction with their mothers.

On the other side, 40.0 per cent daughters of working mothers have a positive and healthy interaction with their mothers, whereas 40.9 per cent daughters of working mothers are falling into the moderate category and 19.1 per cent daughters of working mothers don't have positive interaction with their mothers. The observed value of $\square^2$ was non-significant at 5.0 per cent level of significance.

Table 5.26 Frequency distribution of sharing of experiences and activities by the daughters to their mothers

Experiences	Working mothers' daughters		Non-working mothers' daughters	
	Frequency	Percentage	Frequency	Percentage
High	48	43.6	32	29.1
Medium	40	36.4	38	34.5
Low	22	20.0	40	36.4
Total	110	100.0	110	100.0
χ^2	8.476*		$P < 0.05$	

Table 5.26 shows that 29.1 per cent daughters of non-working mothers share all their experiences and activities with their mothers whereas 34.5 per cent daughters of non-working mothers are falling into moderate category and 36.4 per cent daughters of non-working mothers do not shared their experiences with their mothers.

On the other side, 43.6 per cent daughters of working mothers share all their experiences with their mothers whereas 36.4 per cent daughters of non-working mothers are falling into the moderate category and 20.0 per cent daughters of working mothers do not share their experiences with their mothers. The observed value of χ^2 (8.476*) was significant at 5.0 per cent level of significance.

Table 5.27 Frequency distribution of daughters' openness regarding her friends to their mothers

Experiences	Working mothers' daughters		Non-working mothers' daughters	
	Frequency	Percentage	Frequency	Percentage
Open	70	63.6	58	52.7
Not so open	16	14.5	24	21.8
Not aware	24	21.8	28	25.5
Total	110	100.0	110	100.0
χ^2	3.033		$P > 0.05$	

It is clear from Table 5.27 that 52.7 per cent daughters of non-working mothers are open and frank to their mothers and their mothers are aware about their friends. Whereas, 63.6 per cent daughters of working mothers feel they are open to their mothers and their mothers are aware about all their friends. While about 25.5 per cent daughters of non-working mothers and 21.8 per cent daughters of working mothers feel that, their mothers are not aware about their friends. There is hardly any difference on openness relations between working and non-working mothers. It depends on individual mother that what relations she is having with her daughter, where her daughter can not hide any activity with her mother. In so many studies, it has been found that due to healthy relations, daughter do not hide anything with her mother. In some studies, it has also been seen that daughters used to hide certain things with her mother. So, there is no comparison between working and non-working mothers in openness relations.

The ideal open communication between teenagers and their parents was clearly important to the respondents in this study and was particularly noticeable in teenagers' accounts of their changing relationships with their parents. Their accounts predominantly referred, as Mandy Dent's above, to the sharing of secrets, disclosure and honesty. What exactly did respondents mean by an 'open' relationship? Within the context of the renegotiation of parent-child relationships, 'being open' was used to signify two interdependent goals; the closeness of the relationship in terms of intimacy, and – importantly – the possibility of equality between parent and child.

Closeness was associated with companionship, something that respondents perceived as increasingly possible as children became physically and emotionally mature and potentially capable of a more reciprocal friendship with a parent. This was particularly (but not exclusively) so in same gender parent-teenager pairs. Friendship relies on a reciprocity, which includes mutual disclosure, and many respondents invoked this type of relationship as an ideal in changing parent-child relationships.

Mutual disclosure brings about a more equal status between friends, and parent-teenager relationships are described as potentially attaining the status of friendship as a result. Thus the relationships with her parents as moving into a new equality because she talks to them more openly about personal things. Relationships between teenagers and their parents are characterized by a renegotiation of control over the child's life, which incorporates issues regarding their choices, identity and independence. In common with discourses of democracy and intimacy, talk is perceived to be the most important marker of teenager-parent communication and indicator of closeness. The ultimate marker of independence is perhaps talk about growing up and sexuality, which symbolizes a high degree of intimacy between parents and their teenagers, in addition to representing the child's transition to becoming, in this respect, an equal in the eyes of adults. Some parents and teenagers referred to conversations about sexual matters as indicative of the close nature of their relationships. In a few noteworthy cases, they pointed in particular to the significance of such conversations between fathers and daughters, perhaps because they run counter to gender role expectations and therefore represent closeness all the more forcibly. In the context of a discussion about who his daughter goes to when she is upset.

The observed value of χ^2 is 3.033 per cent is significant at 5.0 per cent level of significance.

Table 5.28 Frequency distribution of daughters view regarding parenting styles

Parenting	Working mothers' daughters		Non-working mothers' daughters	
	Frequency	Percentage	Frequency	Percentage
Good parenting	68	61.8	31	28.2
Average parenting	28	25.5	59	53.6
Low parenting	14	12.7	20	18.2
Total	110	100.0	110	100.0
χ^2	25.933*		P < 0.05	

Table 5.28 shows that 28.2 per cent daughters of non-working mothers are highly satisfied with their parenting styles practiced by their parents, 53.6 per cent daughters of non-working mothers are falling into moderate category and 18.2 per cent daughters of non-working mothers are not satisfied with their parenting styles practised by her parents.

On the other side, 61.8 per cent daughters of working mothers are satisfied with their parenting styles practiced by their parents, 25.5 per cent daughters of working mothers are falling into moderate category and 12.7 per cent daughters of working mothers are not satisfied with their parenting styles practiced by her parents.

Goldberry and Greenberger (1989) supported the statement that employed mothers who value their parenting role are more likely to use authoritative child rearing and encourage greater responsibility and independence.

The value of χ^2 is 25.933* is significant at 5.0 per cent level of significance.

Table 5.29 Frequency distribution of daughters view regarding her career/career aspiration

Parenting	Working mothers' daughters		Non-working mothers' daughters	
	Frequency	Percentage	Frequency	Percentage
High	83	75.5	60	54.5
Moderate	16	14.5	34	30.9
Least	11	10.0	16	14.6
Total	110	100.0	110	100.0
χ^2	11.105*		$P < 0.05$	

Table 5.29 shows that 54.5 per cent non-working mother's daughters are concerned and conscious about their career whereas, 30.9 per cent non-working mother's daughters are falling into moderate category and 14.6 per cent non-working mothers are least concerned about their career.

On the other side, 75.5 per cent working mother's daughters is concerned and conscious about their career whereas 14.5 per cent working mothers' daughters are falling under moderate category.

The observed value of χ^2 is 11.105* is significant at 5.0 per cent level of significance.

TO UNDERSTAND INTERPERSONAL RELATIONSHIP BETWEEN MOTHERS AND GIRLS

Table 5.30 reveals that daughters of non-working mothers are affectionate with their parents and can do anything for their parents and according to them their parents love them more than anything else with a mean score of 0.975 and their father devotes enough time in respect to their mothers and pay much more attention to them and they believe that their mothers are fulfilling their duties well with a mean score of 0.950.

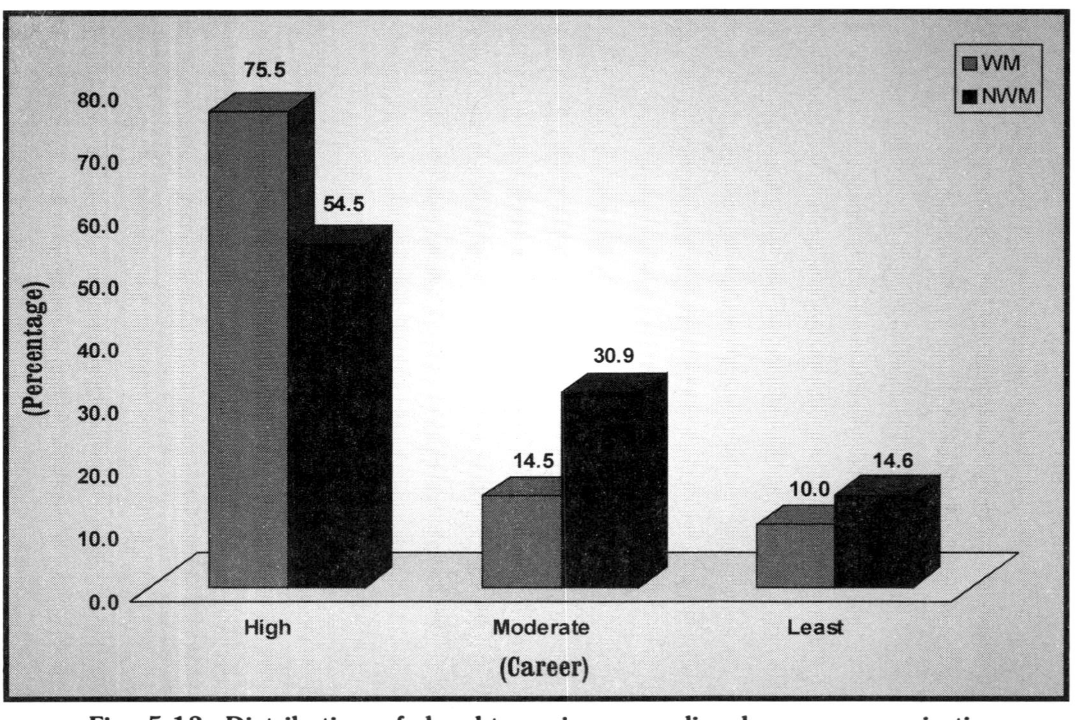

Fig. 5.13: Distribution of daughters view regarding her career aspiration

Table 5.30 Rank-wise distribution of the statement according to the relationship of adolescent girls with her parents

Statement	Working mothers' daughters		Non-working mothers' daughters	
	Mean score	Rank	Mean score	Rank
Parents love you dearly	0.975	I	0.925	IV
Affectionate with the parents	0.975	I	1.000	I
Anything can be done for parents	0.975	I	0.975	II
Father devotes time	0.950	II	0.975	II
Fathers pays more attention	0.950	II	0.925	IV
Mother fulfill duties well	0.950	II	0.975	II
Parents keen towards academics	0.925	III	0.950	III
Parents regularly visit school	0.925	III	0.925	IV
Parents attentive towards fulfilling needs	0.875	IV	0.925	IV
Parents are too demanding at times	0.875	IV	1.000	I
r	0.8821*		$P < 0.05$	

When a daughter is born, there is always the question of how much she will be like her mother. Mothers usually expect boys to be different from them and at unconscious levels, expect their daughters to be like them. However, when the daughters are different, it may be necessary to let go of pre-existing expectations in order to get to know the child they have to see her as she really is, as a person in her own right. Once they are grown, mothers have to let go of their daughters.

Mothers watch their daughters with dread. They worry about their daughter's survival physically, their sexual survival, social survival, personal survival, and relationship survival. Mothers watch their daughters with high hopes that daughters will overcome any difficulties they themselves experienced and hope that their daughters will be more successful. They also hope that they will be able to follow-through with creating a next generation and the survival of the species and family traditions.

One of the most powerful themes in accounts of mother-daughter relationships in western culture has been that of connection and loss. Typically, a daughter's marriage (or desire for a man) threatens the primary and intense bond between her mother and herself. Saying one thing about sex and motherhood, feeling contrary emotions about both at the same time, mother presents an enigmatic picture to her daughter. The first lie – the denial that a woman's sexuality may be in conflict with her role as a mother – is so upsetting to traditional ideas of femininity that it cannot be talked about.

However, a mother does teach her daughter to be dependent. Mothers are seen to reach their daughter to meet men's needs and suppress their own. Girls are taught to be attractive and caring, not to outshine men intellectually and to look for approval. Thus, each mother has to transmit the rules of femininity to her daughter to help them survive in the world, as she knows it. Most mothers are encouraging of their daughters within their mother-daughter relationships, they want to be helpful to their daughters, and feel very bewildered by them. One of the things observed quite regularly is that the mother knows so very little about her own self, that she is giving too much importance on how her daughter turns out to be.

Understanding the mother-daughter relationship is critical to young adult girls because a daughter bonds with her mother in a complex, interdependent association that often inhibits a daughter from establishing her own identity. Many theories have focused on the uniqueness of the mother-daughter relationship. Some of the sociological literature describes the strong bond between mother and daughter as one inhibiting the daughter from establishing her own identity. The first bonding in infancy is with the mother. Although this initial bonding is true for both sexes, boys break away at an early age to identify with their fathers.

Borges (1986) supported the statement that daughters of non-employed mothers had closer relationship with their fathers, perceived them as happier and friendly.

The relationship between daughters of both non-working and working mothers with their parents is significant.

Table 5.31: Rank-wise distribution of the statement according to the relationship of adolescent girls with her peers

Statement	Non-working mothers' daughters		Working mothers' daughters	
	Mean score	Rank	Mean score	Rank
Comfortable fitting in peer group	0.900	II	0.975	I
Spend enough time with peers	0.625	IV	0.900	III
Bulled in peer group	0.500	V	0.750	IV
Peer acceptance necessary	0.825	III	0.925	II
Tried to change to fit in group	0.400	VII	0.600	VI
Happy with your peer group	0.900	II	0.975	I
Share good relation with both sexes	0.825	III	0.925	II
Share friendly and cooperative relations	0.975	I	0.975	I
Peer group influenced	0.475	VI	0.675	V
r	0.8811*		$P < 0.05$	

Table 5.31 shows that daughters of non-working mothers share friendly and cooperative relations with their peers with a mean score of 0.975 and they feel comfortable fitting in their group and they are happy and satisfied with their peer group with a mean score of 0.900.

On the contrary, daughters of working mothers share friendly and cooperative relations with their peer group and are comfortable fitting with their peer group with a mean score of 0.975 and they share good relations with both sexes with a mean score of 0.925.

Daughters of employed mothers have been found to be more independent, particularly in interaction with their peers in a school setting, and to score higher on socio-emotional adjustment measures. .

The value of correlation coefficient 0.8811* is significant between daughters of working and non-working mothers.

Table 5.32 Rank-wise distribution of the statement according to the responsibility of household on daughters

Statement	Non-working mothers' daughters		Working mothers' daughters	
	Mean score	Rank	Mean score	Rank
Responsibility of household on mothers	0.975	II	0.725	V
Family members contribute in work	0.725	V	0.700	VI
Responsibility of home on one's shoulder	0.900	III	0.950	II
Mother force to spend time in house work	0.900	III	0.775	IV
Mother available to serve hot meals	1.000	I	0.650	VII
Responsibility of looking after siblings	0.850	IV	0.975	I
Not able to concentrate on studies	0.900	III	0.950	II
Mother provides time for studies	1.000	I	0.925	III
r	0.1136*		$P < 0.05$	

It is clear from Table 5.32 that daughters of non-working mothers are available to serve hot meals and their mother provides enough time for studies with a mean score of 1.000 and they believe that the responsibility of household lies entirely on their mothers with a mean score of 0.975.

On the contrary, daughters of working mothers have the responsibility of looking after their sibling with a mean score of 0.975 and they also find that the responsibility of home lies on their shoulders and they are not able to concentrate on their studies due to work with a mean score of 0.950.

Girls with employed mothers were more likely than girls whose mothers were full-time homemakers to indicate that women as well as men could do the activities that are usually associated with men; that is, employed mothers' daughters saw women as more competent in the traditionally male domain than the homemakers' daughters did. This result held for girls in two-parent homes and girls in one-parent homes. For boys, however, employment status was not related to the measure of women's competence to do male activities. On the other hand, in two-parent families, both sons and daughters of employed mothers felt that men could do the female activities, while those with full-time homemakers did not, but this was true only in two-parent families. Subsequent analysis showed that the reason it was only found in two parent families is that, it was carried by the fact that, in the two parent families, fathers' with employed wives were more active in traditionally female tasks and in child care. Thus, maternal employment was linked to the less stereotyped view of what men can do because of the effect of maternal employment on the father's role and, in the absence of a father, the effect did not occur.

Gennetian (2002) also supported the statement that due to increase in maternal employment adolescents took on adult roles like caring of siblings etc.

We can conclude from the Table 5.33 that non-working mothers' daughters feel that their mothers are readily available when they require them and the interaction between them is healthy and positive one with a mean score of 0.975 and they believe that they are getting less affectionate with their mothers, due to her tight schedule and when they experienced menarche someone was their to support them with a mean score of 0.900.

Table 5.33 Rank-wise distribution of the statement according to the patterns of interaction between daughters and their mothers

Statement	Non-working mothers' daughters		Working mothers' daughters	
	Mean score	Rank	Mean score	Rank
Mother available when required	0.975	I	0.900	III
Interaction is positive one	0.975	I	0.825	V
Mother gives better advice	0.875	III	0.900	III
Getting less affection due to tight schedule	0.900	II	0.625	VI
Experienced menarche, someone supported	0.900	II	1.000	I
Mothers are daughters best friend	0.800	V	0.925	II
Satisfied with time mother spends	0.825	IV	0.500	VII
Prior knowledge related to menarche provided	0.725	VI	0.850	IV
Emotionally secure when with mother	0.800	V	0.925	II
r	0.7103*		P < 0.05	

On the contrary, working mothers' daughters say that when they experienced menarche someone was there to support and guide them with a mean score of 1.000 they believe mothers are their best friends and they feel emotionally secure, when they are with their mothers with a mean score of value of 0.925.

The value of correlation coefficient (0.7103*) is significant between daughters of working and non-working mothers.

PATTERNS OF INTERACTION BETWEEN MOTHERS AND GIRLS

Table 5.34 Rank-wise distribution of the statement according to the sharing of problems, experiences and activities with mothers

Statement	Non-working mothers' daughters		Working mothers' daughters	
	Mean score	Rank	Mean score	Rank
Gone for smoking, alcohol, drugs	0.925	I	0.950	I
Share experiences with mother	0.550	V	0.825	III
Mother listens to problems	0.825	III	0.875	II
Dating is healthy these days	0.225	VIII	0.550	V
Share every secret with mother	0.450	VII	0.775	IV
When in bad mood, share problem	0.675	IV	0.825	III
Mother shares all problems	0.525	VI	0.425	VI
Feel relaxed after sharing worries	0.875	II	0.800	IV
r	0.7935*		P < 0.05	

A parent's anxiety about the problems that confront his or her adolescent son or daughter is intensified if these problems touch on unresolved problems of his or her own. Probably every parent, to some degree, is vulnerable on this score. Adolescents face issues of sex, so do a great many seemingly "well-adjusted" parents. Adolescents must make decisions with regard to the work they will do in adult life; many parents feel regret about, or dissatisfaction, with, the occupational choices they made. It is important for an ambitious adolescent to prepare himself or herself to get ahead; in the parent population, there are vast numbers of persons who are vigorously competing and endlessly trying to get ahead. Adolescents of marriageable age must make choices as to the person they wish to marry; judging from divorce statistics and studies of marital discord, a large proportion of parents apparently have second thoughts as to whether they made the right choice.

Table 5.34 depicts that daughters of both working and non-working mothers have gone for smoking, alcohol and drugs and according to them their mothers are aware about their activities as they share it with them with a mean score of 0.950 and 0.925, respectively. Non-working mother's daughters have given second rank to the statement that they feel relaxed after sharing their worries with a mean score of 0.875 on the other hand, working mothers' daughters feel that their mother patiently listens to their problems and provide solution to them with a mean score of 0.875.

Parenting teen girls is a huge challenge today and requires patience and perseverance. Making aware a teenager girl who is at high risk for behaviours such as drug/alcohol use, dropping out of school, pregnancy, violence, depression, or suicide is a matter of concern. One of the difficulties parents face is how to recognize the subtle indicators of these behaviours and then how to intervene.

Obstacles that can cause parents to delay getting help for their teen are confusion, denial, and hoping the problem will just go away by itself. Many parents find themselves comparing their child to other children. Although it is tempting to compare the teen to other children, this does not help solve the problem. Parents will do best if they look at their individual situation and then decide on a course of action. Parents should trust their instincts and take action before the situation deteriorates.

Teenager girls experience significant changes during this time (physical, sexual, emotional, and behavioural). Strong guidance is needed from parents and teachers in order to help guide a teen through these stressful new experiences.

Open communication regarding emerging sexual feelings and confusion about the changing relationship among peers is crucial and helps the teen realize that what they are experiencing is normal. Teenager girls grow up too fast these days and they should not be pressured into growing up before they are emotionally ready. They should be allowed to develop their skills in an age appropriate way.

Some differences between the problems mothers attribute to boys as compared with girls were found in a study. The items showing generally small, but consistent, sex differences between characterizations of boys and girls. Boys were characterized as being vigorous, restless, and competitive more often than girls. Girls, on the other hand were more often depicted as being neat, fussy, non-competitive, and sensitive.

Furthermore, boys were described more often than girls as manifesting antisocial behaviour. They live more often, take things, break things, and bully others. "A parents' opinion matters. Mother and fathers are critical role models and should let their attitudes against drug use be known. It's also important to keep an eye on their child's social circle, since, especially for girls, it's their friends who are so central to influencing their behaviour." "At the same time, parents can do things that reduce their child's risk for using drugs, such as teaching them to set goals and assert themselves."

The value of correlation coefficient (0.7935*) is significant between daughters of working and non-working mothers.

From Table 5.35 we can conclude that daughters of both non-working and working mothers have given first rank to the statement that their mothers are aware about all their friends with a mean score of 0.925 and 0.900, respectively and following this is that their mother like their company of friends and are satisfied with their peers with a mean score of 0.850 and 0.825, respectively.

The value of correlation coefficient (0.8951*) is significant between daughters of working and non-working mothers.

Table 5.35: Rank-wise distribution of the statement according to the sharing of peer group of daughters with their mothers as per daughters

Statement	Non-working mothers' daughters		Working mothers' daughters	
	Mean score	Rank	Mean score	Rank
Mothers awareness about all friends	0.925	I	0.900	I
Mother like company of friends	0.850	II	0.825	II
Mothers disliking towards some friends	0.700	III	0.725	IV
Situation to choose family or friends	0.650	IV	0.700	V
Friends share better relation with their mother	0.700	III	0.775	III
r	0.8951*		P < 0.05	

It is clear from Table 5.36 that the daughters of non-working mothers believe that their family holds confidence in them with the highest mean score of 0.975 while the daughters of working mothers say that they are easily given permission to stay at friends home with the highest mean score of 1.000 and they often warned about their returning time when they attend a party.

There are four named parenting styles with fairly predictable outcomes. Authoritative or affirmative parents set limits and boundaries on their teen's behaviour. They are emotionally connected with their kids and are engaged in the parent-child relationship. Liberal or permissive parents often want to be seen as a "friend" rather than an authoritative figure in their child's lives. They let their teens make their own mistakes and don't offer much counsel when mistakes are made. Dominating or authoritarian parents set strict rules and guidelines and show little compassion toward their children. They often micromanage their teens and offer little opportunity for their children to make their own choices. Unengaged parents provide no limits or structure and are not connected with their kids at any level. The authoritative or affirmative parenting style is resoundingly the most successful. Children parented with these ideals are typically successful in academics and socially. The other parenting styles may produce success in academics or social endeavours, but there is usually a consequence of drug, alcohol use and involvement with sex at an early age. Teens parented by an authoritarian method are typically successful academically and are not involved in drugs, alcohol or sex but are often unhappy. Evaluation can adjust parenting strategies to communicate rules and ideals while still providing your teenager choices which they are developmentally ready to handle.

Table 5.36 Rank-wise distribution of the statement according to the daughters view regarding parenting styles

Statement	Non-working mothers' daughters		Working mothers' daughters	
	Mean score	Rank	Mean score	Rank
Family holds confidence	0.975	I	0.975	II
Morals, values, ethics imbibed are good	0.925	III	0.975	II
Given permission to stay at friends home	0.950	II	1.000	I
Consult mother before taking decision	0.925	III	0.750	VII
Mothers become tough when rules are broken	0.925	III	0.925	IV
Mother interferes too much	0.875	IV	0.875	V
Warned about time when attend party	0.850	V	1.000	I
Obey mothers as she is strict	0.775	VII	0.800	VI
Parents overreact when not required	0.725	VIII	0.950	III
r	0.4158*		$P < 0.05$	

The value of the correlation coefficient (0.4158*) is significant at 5.0 per cent hence view of daughters regarding parenting styles were significant.

Table 5.37 Rank-wise distribution of the statement according to the daughters view regarding their career

Statement	Non-working mothers' daughters		Working mothers' daughters	
	Mean score	Rank	Mean score	Rank
Parents guide to pursue some career	0.975	II	1.000	I
Work after marriage	0.925	IV	1.000	I
Working helps to develop personality	1.000	I	1.000	I
Male dominance exists	0.700	VI	0.925	III
Working provides confidence	1.000	II	1.000	I
Insecure about future	0.725	VI	0.775	V
Role of mother is difficult	0.950	III	0.975	II
Perceive mother as role model	0.700	VI	0.900	IV
Adolescence is period of transition	0.975	II	1.000	I
Clear about goals	0.600	VIII	0.400	VI
Recognisation in society	0.950	III	1.000	I
Maternal employment provides status	0.900	V	1.000	I
Parents expectations are high	0.600	VII	0.500	I
Prefer to take career after marriage	0.950	III	1.000	I
r	0.8849		P < 0.05	

The results which from Table 5.37 shows that the daughters of non-working mothers believed that working helps to develop personality and it provides confidence with the highest mean score of 1.000 and on the other hand daughters of working mothers feel that their parents guide them to pursue some career and they believe that working helps to develop one's personality and they would definitely like to work after marriage with a highest mean score of 1.000.

Definite patterns have emerged, some of which are positive. For instance, there's evidence that girls can benefit from maternal employment. Having working mums tends to give girls a boost to self-esteem which pushes them on to greater educational attainment, said much of the earlier research. More recently the issue has turned out to be more complex with the positive effect applying mainly to mothers who are happy to be working. When mothers are stressed or unhappy about their dual roles the children are less likely to do so well, just as children with mothers unhappy at home may fail to achieve their potential. And then there is the off-quoted finding that children of employed mothers often have better academic results than children with homemaker mothers.

Table 5.38 Rank-wise distribution of the statement according to the responsibility of household working and non-working mothers

Statement	Non-working mothers' daughters		Working mothers' daughters	
	Mean score	Rank	Mean score	Rank
Time devotion to family	0.97	I	0.97	I
Domestic workload	0.87	II	0.70	V
Fulfilling needs of family	0.85	III	0.82	III
Support teenager family	0.87	II	0.95	II
Assistance from family	0.47	V	0.80	IV
Daughter helps in work	0.80	IV	0.67	VI
Make sure daughters works	0.75	VI	0.47	IX
Exhaust burst anger	0.85	III	0.50	VIII
Over burdened with work	0.87	II	0.52	VII
r	0.4871		$P < 0.05$	

Hoffman (1974) supported statement that daughters of employed mothers are likely to be independent and to plan future employment.

The value of correlation coefficient (0.8819*) is significant between daughters of non-working and working mothers.

When the responsibility of household on mother was being found, it was found that both working and non-working mothers devote enough time to their families with a mean score of 0.97 followed by domestic workload on non-working mothers with a mean score of 0.87 as well as it was revealed that non-working mothers get enough support from family with a mean score of 0.87 and they feel overburdened with work. On the contrast, it was found working mothers get enough support from family with a mean score of 0.97.

Table 5.39 Rank-wise distribution of the statement according to the interaction between working and non-working mothers with their daughters

Statement	Non-working mothers' daughters		Working mothers' daughters	
	Mean score	Rank	Mean score	Rank
Devote enough time to daughter	0.92	IV	0.90	IV
Know daughter better	1.00	II	0.95	III
Thought of spending extra time	0.82	V	0.65	VII
Quality of quantity time	0.97	III	1.00	I
Healthy interaction	1.00	II	0.82	V
Experienced emotional distances	1.30	I	0.42	VIII
Readily available	0.97	III	0.97	II
Daily invest time	0.97	III	0.75	VI
r	-0.5480		P < 0.05	

Table 5.39 reveals that non-working mothers experienced emotional distances between them and their daughters due to pubertal changes with a mean score of 1.30 followed by it was

non-working mothers know their daughter better than they know themselves and they think they have positive and healthy interaction with their daughters with a mean score of 1.00.

On the contrast, it was found that working mothers think that it is essential to spend quality time rather than quantity with a mean score of 1.00 and they thought they are readily available to their daughters at times of need, with a mean score of 0.97.

Fisher (1939) supported the statement that working mothers spend quality hours with their children on average as the homemakers did.

Steinberg (1990) supported the statement that changes in family relationships during adolescent years are often characterized by increase in both conflict and emotional distance between parents and their adolescent children.

Table 5.40 Rank-wise distribution of the statement according to the mothers listening to the experiences, activities and problems of their daughters

Statement	Non-working mothers' daughters		Working mothers' daughters	
	Mean score	Rank	Mean score	Rank
Hold confidence	1.00	I	1.00	I
Daughters share problem	0.87	V	0.75	V
Sit and talk about problem	0.97	II	0.95	II
Support inter caste marriage	0.32	X	0.45	VII
Share dating experiences	0.42	IX	0.32	VIII
Daughter frank	0.92	III	0.85	III
Mother share problem	0.57	VIII	0.60	VI
Daughter concerned about looks	0.90	IV	0.95	II
Mother select clothing	0.85	VI	0.80	IV
Daughter likes taste	0.67	VII	0.60	VI
r	0.9476**		$P < 0.05$	

Table 5.40 reveals that non-working mothers hold confidence in their daughters with a mean score of 1.00 and they sit and talk about their daughter's problem with a mean score of 0.97.

Similarly, it was found that working mothers also hold confidence in their daughters with a mean score of 1.00 and they also sit and talk about their daughters problem with a mean score of 0.95 and they agreed that their daughter have become concerned about their looks with a mean score of 0.95.

The value of correlation coefficient (0.9476) is significant between non-working and working mothers.

Table 5.41 Rank-wise distribution of the statement according to the mothers awareness and views regarding daughter's friends

Statement	Non-working mothers' daughters		Working mothers' daughters	
	Mean score	Rank	Mean score	Rank
Aware about all friends	1.00	I	0.97	I
Satisfied with peer group	0.95	III	0.87	III
Change her friends	0.80	V	0.90	II
Like all her friends	0.87	IV	0.85	IV
Socialization important	0.97	II	0.97	I
r	0.6176		P < 0.05	

From Table 5.41, we can see that non-working mothers are aware about all friends of their daughters with a mean score of 1.00 and they thought it is important to socialize as it influences adolescents with a mean score of 0.97.

Similarly, it was found that working mothers are also aware about all friends of their daughters and they also found that it is important to socialize with a mean score of 0.97 followed by working mothers also felt that their daughters should change their friends with a mean score of 0.90.

Most mothers said that they talk to their children about sex, including issues such as birth control and the consequences of having sex. Nevertheless, mothers' awareness of their teens' sex lives are frequently inaccurate. When teenagers reported that they had not had sexual intercourse, their mothers were almost always correct in their assessment. But when teens reported that they were having sex, their mothers had only a 50 per cent chance of being right in their assessment. A combination of negative mother-daughter relationships and low blood levels of serotonin, an important brain chemical for mood stability, may be lethal for adolescent girls, leaving them vulnerable to engage in self-harming behaviours such as cutting themselves. The relationship between the level of mother-daughter conflict and self-harming behaviour was not strong. There was a strong relationship between serotonin levels and self-harming behaviour. But when both factors were considered together, the relationship to self-harming behaviours was very strong. "Most people think in terms of biology or environment rather than biology and environment working together," he said. "Having a low level of serotonin is a biological vulnerability for self-harming behaviour and that vulnerability increases remarkably when it is paired with maternal conflict."

From Table 5.42, it has been found that non-working mothers are happy and satisfied by the way they have brought up their daughter with a mean score of 1.000 and others warn their daughters about their returning time when they attend a party followed by mothers are aware of what daughters are doing at their back with a mean score of 0.975.

On the contrary, working mothers supervise their daughters activities with a mean score of 1.00 as well as they are happy the way they have brought up their daughters followed by mothers ensure about returning time which daughters go to party with a mean score of 0.975.

Table 5.42: Rank wise distribution of the statement according to the mothers way of disciplining their daughters

Statement	Non-working mothers' daughters		Working mothers' daughters	
	Mean score	Rank	Mean score	Rank
Freedom provided to daughter	0.925	IV	0.825	VI
Aware about what happens at back	0.975	II	0.975	II
Happy the way brought up	1.000	I	1.000	I
Child is wise, mature	0.575	VIII	0.850	V
Regret upon parenting style	0.925	IV	0.875	IV
Child can adjust in situation	0.725	VII	0.850	V
Enough privacy	0.925	IV	0.850	V
Adjustments are made	0.875	V	0.850	V
Supervise daughters activities	0.950	III	1.000	I
Daughters independent to look for herself	0.725	VII	0.875	IV
Attends party returning time ensured	1.000	I	0.975	II
Neither child nor adult	0.975	II	0.975	II
Rules are necessary for discipline	0.950	III	0.925	III
Enough freedom to do anything	0.850	VI	0.925	III
r	0.6032*		P < 0.05	

Teenagers experiencing with hormonal changes and an ever-complex world, may feel that no one can understand their feelings, especially parents. As a result, the teen may feel angry, alone and confused while facing complicated issues about identity, peers, sexual behaviour, drinking and drugs. Parents may be frustrated and angry that the teen seems to no longer respond to parental authority. Methods of discipline that worked well in earlier years may no longer have an effect. And, parents may feel frightened and helpless about the choices their teen in making. Dealing with the issues of adolescence can be trying for all concerned. But families are generally successful at helping their children accomplish the developmental goals of the teen years – reducing dependence on parents, while becoming increasingly responsible and independent.

Powell (1960) supported the statement and found that there was no difference in attitude towards child rearing between working and non-working mothers.

The value of correlation coefficient (0.6032) is significant between working and non-working mothers.

Table 5.43 Rank wise distribution of the statement according to the mothers views regarding career

Statement	Non-working mothers' daughters		Working mothers' daughters	
	Mean score	Rank	Mean score	Rank
Check academic performance	0.92	IV	0.82	VI
Regularly visit school	0.97	II	0.97	II
Ensure enough time given to studies	1.00	I	1.00	I
Support to choose any vocation	0.57	VIII	0.85	V
Provide guidance	0.92	IV	0.87	IV
Getting into profession	0.72	VII	0.85	V
Children of working mothers are independent	0.92	IV	0.85	V
Work provides confidence	0.87	V	0.85	V
Financial crisis affected	0.95	III	1.00	I
Egalitarian attitudes	0.72	VII	0.87	IV
Working provides status	1.00	I	0.97	II
Work after marriage	0.97	II	0.97	II
Women self-contained	0.95	III	0.92	III
Male dominance exists	0.85	VI	0.92	III
r	0.6032*		$P < 0.05$	

Table 5.43 reveals that non-working mothers ensure that their daughters give enough time to studies with a mean score of 1.000 and they also believe that work provides some status to a women and many non-working mothers would like their daughters to work after marriage with a mean score of 0.97. On the contrary, working mothers think that financial crisis have affected the daughters decision in deciding up the career with a mean score 1.000 and they too ensure that enough time is given to studies followed by working mothers feels that working provides status as well as they would like their daughters to work after marriage with a mean score of 0.97. Daughters of employed mothers have been found to have higher academic achievement, greater career success, more non-traditional career choices, and greater occupational commitment.

The value of correlation coefficient (0.6032*) is significant between non-working mothers and working mothers.

Table 5.44 Relationship between non-working mother and their daughters

Section	Non-working mothers'		Daughters	
	Mean score	Rank	Mean score	Rank
A	7.65	1.12	16.72	2.64
B	7.30	0.88	10.77	2.56
B_1	7.55	1.15	5.05	1.81
B_2	4.60	0.81	3.67	1.47
B_3	12.40	1.51	14.32	2.67
C	15.60	1.60	11.95	1.62

Table 5.44 shows that the mean score was the highest in the area of section C in case of non-working mothers and in case of daughters, it was the highest in the area of section A.

Table 5.45 reveals that the mean score was the highest in the area of section C in case of working mothers and in case of daughters, it was the highest in the area of section A.

Table 5.45 Relationship between working mother and their daughters

Section	Non-working mothers'		Daughters	
	Mean score	Rank	Mean score	Rank
A	6.67	1.82	18.22	2.34
B	6.47	1.26	10.62	2.03
B_1	7.27	1.97	6.05	1.75
B_2	4.52	1.15	3.93	1.70
B_3	12.75	1.35	16.20	2.51
C	15.42	0.98	12.47	0.78

Table 5.46 Correlation coefficient between family variables and relationship with working, non-working and teenagers

Variables	Correlation coefficient	
	Relationship with working mother	Relationship with non-working mother
Family type	0.1211	0.4126*
Family size	-0.4615	-0.3819
Caste	0.3664*	0.4916*
Economic status	0.4881*	0.5163*
Religion	0.3014*	0.4672*

Table 5.46 shows that correlation coefficient between family variables and relationship with working, non-working mothers and teenager's, relationship of working mothers and girls positively correlated with caste, economic status and religion and negatively correlated with family size (-0.4615). Relationship of non-working mother and teenagers positively correlated with caste (0.4916*), family type (0.4126*), economic status (0.5163*) and religion (0.4672*) and negatively correlated with family size (0.3819).

SUMMARY AND CONCLUSION

Mothers and daughters have a special bond with all its complex emotions – anger, resentment, competition and of course, love. But every son will also hear echoes of his own life with mother. Mothers and daughters – sometimes they're enemies, sometimes best friends.

Mothers it is very important to develop a loving, healthy relationship with yourself. The most loving thing you can do for your daughter is develop a healthier relationship with yourself. A mother is less likely to try to control her daughter's life when she accepts herself (faults and all).

OBJECTIVES

1. To study the socio-demographic people of teenager's girls.

2. To study the nature, attitude and relationship of teenager's with her working and non-working mothers.
3. To identify the responsibility and role of teenager's in household activities with selected mothers.
4. To understand interpersonal relationship with mothers and girls.
5. Patterns of interaction between mother and girls.
   (a) Sharing of experiences and activities
   (b) Knowledge of friends
   (c) Discipline maintained of different level with mothers.
   (d) Personal problems.

RESEARCH METHODOLOGY

The study was conducted in Moradabad district. Total 8 colleges and schools were randomly selected in this study. Total 220 respondents were selected (110 teenager girls' working mothers) and (110 teenager girls' non-working mothers). Dependent and independent variables were used such as age, caste, education, knowledge, awareness, parent-child relationship etc. The statistical tools were used such as S.D, chi-square, correlation coefficient.

MAJOR FINDINGS

1. 47.3 per cent girls of working mother belonged to 17 - 18 years age group followed by 27.3 per cent girl respondents of 15 -16 years age group. 44.6 per cent girls of non-working mother belonged to 17 - 18 years age group followed by 33.6 per cent girls of 15 - 16 years age group. 21.8 per cent girls of non-working mother belonged to 13 - 14 years age group.
2. 50.9 per cent girls belonged to general category of working mother whereas 32.7 per cent girls belonged to OBC category. 41.8 per cent girls were belonged to OBC

category of non-working mother whereas 31.8 per cent girls were from general category. Environment and caste play an important role to interpersonal relationship with working and non-working mothers and girls respondents.

3. 77.7 per cent girls were belonged to Hindu family, whereas 6.8 per cent girls from Muslim family, 8.7 per cent girls were from Sikh religion and only 6.8 per cent girls were from Christian family.
4. 68.2 per cent girls working mother were belonged to nuclear family and 31.8 per cent girls from joint family system. 53.6 per cent girls of non-working mothers were belonged to nuclear family whereas 46.4 per cent girls were from joint family. Family type also plays a crucial role in relationship of mothers and teenaged girls.
5. 52.7 per cent girls of working mother have 2 to 4 members family size whereas 30.0 per cent girls have 5 to 7 members in family. 38.2 per cent girls of non-working mothers have 8 and above family size whereas 33.6 per cent girls of non-working mother have 5 to 7 members in family. Family size is not alone responsible for the kind of relationships that develop among family members. Instead, they depend upon a number of factors, four of which are especially important.

   The larger the family, the greater the number of interactional systems and, normally, the greater the friction in the home, however, friction is often counteracted by the authoritarian discipline of the parents. To avoid the unhealthy home climate that friction gives rise to and to enable each family member to live in harmony with other family members. Parents of large families more often use authoritarian child training methods than do parents of smaller ones.
6. 47.2 per cent girls of working mother have middle economic status while 26.4 per cent girls have lower and higher economic status. 42.7 per cent girls of non-

working mother have lower economic status whereas 40.9 per cent girls have middle economic status. There is much impact of economic status on the relations of mother and teenager girls, because in all the disputes, money plays an important role. Healthy relations are established in high status families.

7. 40.9 per cent women have earned up to Rs. 5,000 monthly, 26.4 per cent women have earned Rs. 5,000 to Rs. 10,000 monthly and 22.7 per cent working women earned Rs. 10,000 to Rs. 15,000 monthly.

8. 34.5 per cent girls of working women have family monthly income Rs. 20,000 to Rs. 30,000 whereas 29.1 per cent girls of working women have family income Rs. 10,000 to Rs. 20,000. 43.6 per cent girls of non-working women have monthly family income Rs. 10,000 to Rs. 20,000 followed by 32.7 per cent were up to Rs. 10,000. 9.1 per cent girls of working women have family income Rs. 30,000 and above whereas 5.5 per cent girls of non-working women.

9. 15-16 years of working mother having mean score 0.89, whereas this relationship is least in age group 17-18 years having mean score of 0.80. In non-working mother daughter the relationship is more and good in age group 13-14 years with mean score (0.86) followed by age group 15-16 years with mean score 0.81, whereas, this relationship is least in age group 17-18 years having mean score of 0.79.

10. 15-16 as its mean score is 0.91 whereas, this relationship is least in age group 13-14 years having mean score of 0.68 and standard deviation 0.19. Relationship of daughters of non-working mothers with her peers according to their age is more in age group 13-14 years with mean score 0.85 whereas, it is least in age group 17-18 years having an mean score of 0.71 and S.D. 0.16. Teenager girls having good relations with family members continue to have same with their peer group. This is

because of family background, which leaves indelible imprint on their children. This continues further and children behave in the same way with group also.

11. 15-16 years having mean score of 0.89 and S.D. 0.17 whereas, it is least in age group of 17-18 years having mean score 0.79 and standard deviation 0.15. Responsibility of household on daughters of non-working mothers according to their age group is more in age group of 13-14 years having mean score 0.91 whereas, this responsibility is least in age group 15-16 (0.87) and 17-18 years having mean score 0.88 and standard deviation (0.17).

12. Interaction between working mother and their daughters according to age group is more in 13-14 years having mean score 0.90 whereas, this interaction is less in age group 17-18 years (0.77) and S.D. (0.20). Interaction between non-working mother and their daughter according to age group is more in age group 13-14 years having mean score (0.91) and these have positive interaction with their mother whereas it is least in age group 17-18 years having mean score (0.75) which shows that they do not have good and positive interaction with their mothers.

13. Career aspiration of daughters of working mothers in accordance to their age is more in age group 13-14 years having mean score of 0.90 whereas, this career aspiration is least in age group 17-18 years having mean score of 0.86 and S.D. (0.09). It is very much clear from the above Table that the daughters of non-working mother are more conscious about their career in the age group 15-16 years having a mean score of 0.91 whereas, the career aspiration is least in the age group 13-14 years having a mean score of 0.82 and S.D. 0.07. Educated and working mother have an important role is selecting career line for teenager girls, which is not possible with non-working mother. Because level of thinking of an

educated and working mother is entirely different from non-working and uneducated mother. They are supposed to be more conscious about the career of her daughter.

14. Sharing of experiences and activities between working mothers and their daughters according to their age group is more in age group 13-14 years having mean (0.83) whereas it is least with age group 17-18 years having mean score of 0.63 and S.D. 0.22. Sharing of experiences and activities between non-working mother and their daughter according to their age group is more in age group 15-16 years having an mean score of 0.80 whereas, this sharing of experiences is least in age group 17-18 years having an mean scores of 0.61 and S.D. 0.24.

15. Working mothers are aware about the friends of her teenager daughter. They seem to be afraid of her daughter about indulgence is bad activities. Puberty age is more sensitive. At this stage, mothers used to have an eye on her daughter's activities like, while talking on telephone, writing letter to friends, checking her room, know the status of friends, her friend's family background, about class studies etc. These she does, because she is educated. Non-working mothers can't do all these.

16. Discipline of daughters of working mothers according to their age is more in age group 15-16 years having mean scores of 0.88 whereas discipline of daughters is least in age group 17-18 years with a mean score of 0.78 and S.D. (0.18). Discipline of daughters of non-working mother with respect to their age group is more in age group 15-16 years having mean score of 0.83 whereas it is least in age group 17-18 years having mean score of 0.74.

17. 46.4 per cent non-working mothers had greater amount of household responsibilities whereas the remaining 44.5 per cent the non-working mothers had moderate amount of household responsibilities. On the contrast, 30.9 per

cent working mothers revealed that they had high amount of household responsibilities and greater majority of about 45.5 per cent working mothers has moderate amount of household responsibility while the remaining 23.6 per cent the working mother showed that they had very less or few household responsibility.

18. 73.6 per cent non-working mothers have a very good, healthy and positive interaction with their daughters whereas 14.5 per cent non-working mothers have moderate amount of interaction with their daughter and the remaining 11.9 per cent non-working mothers have least amount of interaction with their daughters. On the other hand, 47.3 per cent working mothers have a good positive interaction with their daughters, whereas 41.8 per cent working mothers have moderate amount of interaction with their daughters and the remaining 10.9 per cent working mothers have least amount of interaction with their daughters.

19. 45.5 per cent non-working mothers have very good understanding with their daughters and they share their experiences and problem with one another and have a friendly relationship with one another whereas 38.2 per cent non-working mothers have moderate amount of understanding with their daughters and the remaining 16.3 per cent non-working mothers have very less understanding with their daughters and they do not share their experience and problems with one another.

    On the other side, 40.9 per cent working mothers have good understanding with their daughters and they have a friendly relationship with one another whereas 30.9 per cent working mothers have moderate amount of understanding with their daughters and about 28.2 per cent working mothers have less understanding with their daughters and they do not share their experiences and problems with one another, which is quite high in comparison to the non-working mothers.

20. 58.2 per cent non-working mothers have brought up their daughters very good and they are satisfied with it whereas, 31.8 per cent non-working mothers are falling into the moderate category and about 2.7 per cent non-working mothers are not satisfied the manner they have brought up their daughters. On the other side, 65.5 per cent working mothers are highly satisfied by their parenting style whereas 31.8 per cent working mothers are falling into the moderate category.

21. 68.2 per cent non-working mothers are highly concerned about their daughters' career and would like their daughters to take up some career, and would support them. 13.6 per cent non-working mothers are falling into the moderate category and the remaining 18.2 per cent non-working mothers are least concerned about their daughters' career. 75.5 per cent working mothers are highly concerned about their daughters' career whereas, 14.5 per cent working mothers are falling into the moderate category.

22. 56.4 per cent daughters of non-working mothers share or possess good relationship with their parents whereas 29.1 per cent daughters of non-working mothers are falling into the moderate category and 14.5 per cent daughters of non-working mothers do not share a good relationship with their parents. On the contrast, 67.3 per cent daughters of working mothers possess good relationship with their parents. 20.0 per cent daughters of working mothers are falling into the moderate category and 12.7 per cent daughters of working mothers does not share a good relationship with their parents.

23. 47.3 per cent daughters of non-working mothers have average relationship with their peers while 52.7 per cent daughters of working mothers share good relationship with their peers and around 29.1 per cent daughters of non-working mothers do not share good relationship with their peers while on the other side only 16.4 per cent daughters are falling into this category.

24. 72.7 per cent daughters of non-working mothers feel that they have maximum responsibilities of household upon them and only 10.9 per cent daughters feel that they have least responsibilities and 54.5 per cent daughters of working mothers feel they have maximum responsibilities and only 16.4 per cent daughters feel that they have least responsibilities.

25. 34.5 per cent daughters of non-working mothers have a positive and healthy interaction with their mothers whereas 49.1 per cent daughters of non-working mothers are falling into the moderate category whereas, 16.4 per cent daughters of non-working mothers don't have positive interaction with their mothers. On the other side, 40.0 per cent daughters of working mothers have a positive and healthy interaction with their mothers, whereas 40.9 per cent daughters of working mothers are falling into the moderate category and 19.1 per cent daughters of working mothers do not have positive interaction with their mothers.

26. 29.1 per cent daughters of non-working mothers share all their experiences and activities with their mothers whereas 34.5 per cent daughters of non-working mothers are falling into moderate category and 36.4 per cent daughters of non-working mothers do not shared their experiences with their mothers. On the other side, 43.6 per cent daughters of working mothers share all their experiences with their mothers whereas 36.4 per cent daughters of non-working mothers are falling into the moderate category and 20 per cent daughters of working mothers does not share their experiences with their mothers.

27. 52.7 per cent daughters of non-working mothers are open and frank to their mothers and their mothers are aware about their friends. Whereas, 63.6 per cent daughters of working mothers feel they are open to their mothers and their mothers are aware about all their friends. While

about 25.5 per cent daughters of non-working mothers and 21.8 per cent daughters of working mothers feel that their mothers are not aware about their friends.

28. 28.2 per cent daughters of non-working mothers are highly satisfied with their parenting styles practiced by their parents, 53.6 per cent daughters of non-working mothers are falling into moderate category and 18.2 per cent daughters of non-working mothers are not satisfied with their parenting styles practiced by her parents. On the other side, 61.8 per cent daughters of working mothers are satisfied with their parenting styles practiced by their parents, 25.5 per cent daughters of working mothers are falling into moderate category and 12.7 per cent daughters of working mothers are not satisfied with their parenting styles practiced by her parents.

29. 30.9 per cent non-working mother's daughters are falling into moderate category and 14.6 per cent non-working mothers are least concerned about their career. On the other side, 75.5 per cent working mother's daughters are concerned and conscious about their career whereas 14.5 per cent working mothers' daughters are falling under moderate category.

30. On the contrary, daughters of working mothers share friendly and cooperative relations with their peer group and are comfortable fitting with their peer group with a mean score of 0.975 and they share good relations with both sexes with a mean score of 0.925. Daughters of employed mothers have been found to be more independent, particularly in interaction with their peers in a school setting, and to score higher on socio-emotional adjustment measures.

31. Girls with employed mothers were more likely than girls whose mothers were full-time homemakers to indicate that women as well as men could do the activities that are usually associated with men; that is, employed mothers' daughters saw women as more competent in the

traditionally male domain than the homemakers' daughters did. This result held for girls in two-parent homes and girls in one-parent homes. For boys, however, employment status was not related to the measure of women's competence to do male activities. On the other hand, in two – parent families, both sons and daughters of employed mothers felt that men could do the female activities, while those with full-time homemakers did not, but this was true only in two-parent families. Subsequent analysis showed that the reason it was only found in two parent families is that, it was carried by the fact that, in the two parent families, fathers' with employed wives were more active in traditionally female tasks and in child care.

32. A parent's anxiety about the problems that confront his or her adolescent son or daughter is intensified if these problems touch on unresolved problems of his or her own. Probably every parent, to some degree, is vulnerable on this score. Adolescents face issues in the area of sex, so do a great many seemingly "well-adjusted" parents. Adolescents must make decisions with regard to the work they will do in adult life; many parents feel regret about, or dissatisfaction, with the occupational choices they made. Teenager girls experience significant changes during this time (physical, sexual, emotional, and behavioural). Strong guidance is needed from parents and teachers in order to help guide a teen through these stressful new experiences.

33. Teens parented by an authoritarian method are typically successful academically and are not involved in drugs, alcohol or sex but are often unhappy. Evaluation can adjust your parenting strategies to communicate rules and ideals while still providing your teenager choices which they are developmentally ready to handle.

34. Non-working mothers are aware about all friends of their daughters with a mean score of 1.00 and they thought it

is important to socialize as it influences adolescents with a mean score of 0.97. Similarly, it was found that working mothers are also aware about all friends of their daughters and they also found that it is important to socialize with a mean score of 0.97 followed by working mothers also felt that their daughters should change their friends with a mean score of 0.90.

35. Teenagers dealing with hormonal changes and an ever-complex world, may feel that no one can understand their feelings, especially parents. As a result, the teen may feel angry, alone and confused while facing complicated issues about identity, peers, sexual behaviour, drinking and drugs. Parents may be frustrated and angry that the teen seems to no longer respond to parental authority. Methods of discipline that worked well in earlier years may no longer have an effect.

36. Daughters of employed mothers have been found to have higher academic achievement, greater career success, more non-traditional career choices, and greater occupational commitment.

SUGGESTIONS, RECOMMENDATIONS AND POLICY IMPLICATIONS

1. To improve communication with their moms, girls should choose their battles carefully (confronting their moms only when an issue is valid and important) and find a good time for a talk (not when moms walk in the door after work, after a disturbing phone call, or when she's rushing off to an appointment.

2. Communicating effectively with your teenage daughter is perhaps the most important aspect of your relationship with her. She will listen to you more and accept your guidance if you develop good listening skills. You must practice "active listening" which means that you listen with your eyes, ears, and heart not only to her words, but also to her feelings without interruption or criticism.

3. Encourage your daughter to be assertive so she can speak up for herself when she is not treated respectfully.

4. Encourage your daughter to get a good education and if possible to go to college. Show an interest in her homework, assisting if you can when she needs help.

5. Teach her to set boundaries. This means to set limits about what she will allow another person to say or do to her in a relationship. She needs to say, "No!" when someone is verbally, emotionally, or physically abusive. If the person does not stop, then she needs to leave the relationship.

6. Probably the best and most valued mother-daughter relationship is the friendship kind. Such friendship based interactions between a mother and her daughter is less susceptible to tension and misunderstanding and there will be a lot of room for dialog rather than that of rushing to enforce authority. Both parties share their secrets freely between themselves and girls raised with such an interaction with their mothers tend to grow up to be confident and strong willed.

7. Understand that building a better relationship with each other takes time. It also takes patience and the appropriate resources to help you with this.

BIBLIOGRAPHY

Abraham, S. and Villanueva (2005). Mothers and daughters in conflict: A longitudinal examination of European American, African American and Latina mothers and daughters during the transition to puberty. *Dissertation Abstracts International,* **65**(8-13): 4316.

Andrew, Cooper (2002). Parenting behaviour and adolescents. *Journal of Child Development,* **59**(4): 103-104.

Arendell, T. (1997). "A Social Constructionist Approach to Parenting". pp. 1-44. In: *Contemporary Parenting: Challenges and Issues*, edited by Terry Arendell, Thousand Oaks, CA: Sage.

Becker, P.E. and P. Moen (1999). "Scaling Back: Dual Earner Couples' Work – Family Strategies". *Journal of Marriage and the Family,* **224**(4): 85-100.

Bianchi, S.D. (2000). *The effect of wife's employment on the family power structure*. pp. 347-352.

Bluestone, C. and Tamis – Le Monda (1999). Correlates of parenting styles in predominantly working and middle class mothers. *Journal of Marriage and the Family,* **61**: 881-893.

Blum, R.W. (2002). University of Minnesota Division of General Pediatrics and Adolescent Health, visit http://www.allaboutkids,umn.edu.

Borges, J.M. (1986). Child rearing attitudes of working and non-working mother's psychology. *Journal of Research,* **12:** 54-61.

Bowles, Samuel; Herbert Gintis and Melissa Osborne Groves, eds. (2005). *Unequal chances: Family Background and Economic Success*, New York: Russell Sage Foundation.

Bronfenbrenner, U and Morris P.A. (2005). *The ecology of developmental process, Handbook of child psychology*, Vol. 1 (5th ed., pp. 553-584), New York Wiley.

Brown (1993). Coated into opinion of children regarding their mothers employment. *Indian Journal of Behaviour,* **15**: 5-12.

Camacho, M. and Wanda, I. (1999). The effects of a graduate education on Puerto Rican mother and daughter relationships, Dissertation Abstracts International: Section B, Dec., **60**(5-B): 2332.

Christopher, F.S.; Johnson, and M. Roosa (1993). Family individual and social correlates of early Hispanic adolescent sexual expression. *Journal of Sex Research,* **30**: 54-61.

Crepinsek, Mary Kay and Nancy R. Rurstein (2009). lghelfi@ers.usda.gov.

Crouter, A.C., Manke, B.A. and Mc Hale, S.M. (1990). The family context of gender intensification in early adolescence. *Child Development,* **66**: 317-329.

Dekovic, M.; Noom, M.J. and Meeus, W. (1998). Expectations regarding development during adolescence. Parent and adolescent perceptions. *Journal of Youth and Adolescence,* **26**: 253-271.

Dornbusch, K. (1995). Sex roles, identity, marital power and marital satisfaction among middle class couples in India. *Sex Roles, Journal of Research,* **22**: 289-300.

Duncan, R.J.; Haurin, R.J. and Mott, F.L. (2001). The effects of mothers employment on adolescent and early adult outcomes of young men and women. In C.D. Hayes and S.B. Kamerman (Eds.) Children of working parents experiences and outcomes (pp. 130-219). Washington, D.C.; National Academy Press.

Enberg, Karen (1999). www.prometheusbooks.com.1999 ISBN 1-57392-745-7.

Fisher, B. and J. Tronto (1990). "Towards a Feminist Theory of Caring". Pp. 36-63 in Circles of care: Work and Identity in Women's Lives, edited by Emily K. abel and Margaret K. Nelson. Englewood Cliffs, NJ: Prentice Hall.

Fisher, C.D. and Gitelson, R. (1939). A meta analysis of the correlates of Role conflict and Ambiguity. *Journal of Applied Psychology,* **68**: 320-333.

Furstenberg, Frank F. (2000). "The Sociology of Adolescence and Youth in the 1990s: A Critical Commentary". *Journal of Marriage and the Family,* **62**(4): 896-910.

Garey, A.I. (1999). Weaving Work and Motherhood. Philadelphia: Temple University Press.

Gavin, A. Leslic (1996). JSTOR: Child Development Vol. 67, No. 2 (Apr. 1996) pp. 375-386. http://www.jstor,org./PSS/1131820.

Gennetion, L. (2002). Employment of mothers and their children. *Journal of Research,* **13**: 41-61.

Gottfried, A.E. (1999). Maternal employment in the family setting. Development and environmental issues. In: T.V. Lerner and N.L. Galambos (Eds), *Employment mothers and their children*. pp. 63-84, New York: Garland.

Grader, J.A. and Brooks, G.I. (1999). How mothers and daughters negotiate the transition into adolescence, *Lawrence Erlbaum Associates Publisher,* **XIV**: 362.

Greenberg, E.; and Goldberry, W.A. (1989). Work Parenting and the Socialization of Children Development, *Psychology*, **25:** 25-35.

Gross, P.H. and Mccallum, R. (2000). Operationalization and predictive utility of mother daughter synchrony. *School Psychology Quarterly*, Feb., **15**(3): 279-294.

Hochschild, A.R. (1997). *The Time Bind: When Work Become Home and Home Becomes Work*. New York: Metropolitan Books.

Hochschild, A.R. (1998). "Ideals of Care: Traditional, Postmodern, Cold-Modern, and Warm – Modern." pp. 527-538. In: *Families in the U.S.: Kinship and Domestic Politics*, edited by Karen V. Hansen and Anita Ilta Garey. Philadelphia: Temple University Press.

Hoffman, Wladis Lois (1998). http://parenthood.library.wisc.edu/Hoffman.html.

Hoffman, L.W. (1993). Effects of maternal employment on the child. A review of the research. *Development Psychology*, **10:** 204-228.

Hoffman, L.W. (1998). Effects of maternal employment on the child. A review of the research. *Development Psychology,* **10**: 204-228.

Hoffman, L.W. (2000). Maternal employment: Effects of social context. In: R.D. Taylor and M.C. Wang (Eds), *Resilience across contexts: Family, work culture and community* (pp. 147-176). Mahwah, NJ: Erlbaurn.

Hoffman, L.W. and Nyl. E.Z. (1974). *Working mothers*, San Fransisco, Jersey Bas.

Ilyas, Q.S.M. (1990). Determinants of perceived role conflicts among women. *Sex Roles, Journal of Research*, **22:** 237-247.

Kalen Koski, C.M. and Pabilonia, W.S. (2009). "Does working while in High School/Reduce Study Time in the U.S. ?" *Social Indicators Research*, **93**(1): 117-121.

Kaplan, E.B. (2000). "Using Food as a Metaphor for Care: Middle – School Kids Talk About Family, School, and Class Relationships." *Journal of Contemporary Ethnography*, **29**(4): 474-509.

Kaplan, E.B. and Davidson, C. (2002). "Scheduling, Worrying and Stepping up: Working paper No. 52, May 2002. http://dcollections.bc.edu/R/?func =dbin-jump-full 8 object-id=85854 & local-base=GENOI.

Kiuchi, A. (1997). Independent and interdependent construal of the self, their correlates and conflicts in female college students and their mothers. *Japanese Journal of educational Psychology*, Jan. **45**(2): 183-191.

Lee, E.E. (2000). *Nurturing success: Successful women of colour and their daughters*, Greenwood Publishing Group, Inc, XVIII, 293.

Lewis, J. (2007). Teenagers and their parents: *The Political Quarterly*, **78**(2): 292-300 ISSN0032-3179. http://www.2.lse,ae.uk/research And Expertise/ Expert.

Lloyd, G.W. (1994). Parenting behaviours and parent child relationships. *Development Psychology*, **34**: 1450-1458.

Marshall, Katherine (2007). "The Busy Lives of Teenagers." *Perspectives*; 5-15.

Mates, D. and K.R. Allison (1992). "Sources of Stress and Coping Responses of High School Students". *Adolescence*, **27**(2): 461-474.

Miller, L. Kramer, R. and Warner, V. (1997). Intergenerational transmission of parental bonding among women. *Journal of American Academy of Child and adolescent Psychiatry*, Aug. **36**(8): 1134-1139.

Mills, R.S. (1999). Exploring the effects of law power schemes in mothers. *New Directions for Child and Adolescent Development*, **86**: 61-77.

Moffitt, F.L. (2003). The effects of mothers employment on adolescent and early adult outcomes of young men and women. In: C.D. Hayer and S.B. Kamerman (Eds.). *Children of working parents: Experiences and outcomes* (pp. 130-219). Washington, D.C. National Academy Press.

Morris, D.L. and Ramanan, J. (2001). Effects of early and recent maternal employment on children from low – income families. *Child Development,* **63**: 938-949.

Nock, S.L. and P.W. Kingston (1995). "Time with Children: The Impact of Couples' Work – Time Commitments." *Social Forces,* **67**(3): 59-85.

Paulson, S.E., J.J. Koman III, and J.P. Hill (1990). "Maternal Employment and Parent – Child Relations in Families of Seventh Graders." *Journal of Early Adolescence,* **10**(3): 279-295..

Pecctioni, L.L. and Nussbaum, J.F. (2000). The influence of autonomy and paternalism and communicative behaviours in mother-daughter relationships prior to dependency, *Health Communication*, **12**(4): 317-338.

Porterfield, Shirley, L. and Anne E. Winkler (2007). "Teen Time Use and Parental Education: Evidence from the CPS, MTF, and ATUS". *Monthly Labour Review,* **130**(5): 37-56.

Powell, M.A. and Parecel, T.L. (1960). "Parental work family size and social capital effects on early adolescent educational outcomes." *Research in sociology of Work,* **7**: 1-30.

Powers, S.I. and Wesh, D.P. (1999). Mother daughter interactions and adolescent girls depression, *Lawrence Erlbaum Associates Publishers,* **XIV**: 362.

Price, Joseph; Bijou Hunt; Vanessa Wight; and Suzanne Bianchi (2007). "The Time Use of Teenagers'." Unpublished manuscript.

Richardson, J. (1993). Parental employment and child cognitive development. Unpublished manuscript, National Bureau of Economic Research.

Rower, D. (1991). Parent-child relations and academic achievement. In M.G. Sanders (Ed.), schooling students placed at risk: Research, Policy, and practice in the education of poor and minority adolescents (pp. 65-82) Mahwah, NJ: Erlbaum.

Ruddick, S. (1995). Care as Labour and Relationships. Pp. 23-25 in Norms 'Values: Essay on the Work of Virginia heed. Lanhom, MD: Littlefield Publishers.

Starrels, J. (1992). Working mother a review of research. *Child Development,* **34**: 513-542.

Steinberg, L.D. (1990). Interdependence in the family: Autonomy conflict, and harmony in the parent, adolescent relationship. In S.S. Feldman & G.R. Elliott (Eds), At the threshold: The developing adolescent. (pp. 255-276). Cambridge, M.A.: Harvard University Press.

Tarlow, B. (1996). "Caring: A Negotiated Process that Varies." Pp. 89-117 in Caregiving: Readings in knowledge, Practice, Ethics and Politics, edited by Patricia Benner, Nel Noddings and Susanne Gordon, Philadelphia: University of Pennsylvania Press.

Washington (2002). University of Minnesota Division of General Pediatrics and Adolescent Health, visit. http://www.allaboutkids.umn.edu.

Weiss, H.K.H. Vaughan and P. Mayer, E. (2000). "Low-Income Working Mothers' Negotiate Work, Family, and Children's School". Unpublished paper, Harvard Family Research Project.

INDEX